FROM COPING TO THRIVING

FROM COPING TO THRIVING

HOW TO TURN SELF-CARE INTO A WAY OF LIFE

HANNAH BRAIME

Contents

part 4. Nurturing the Body

part 5. Nurturing the Mind

part 6. Continuing the Journey

Introduction

Welcome to *From Coping to Thriving*. Thank you for purchasing this book, and congratulations on investing in your relationship with yourself. My intention is that this book will provide you with a comprehensive introduction to self-care. In the following pages, you'll find plenty of tips and suggestions that you can use to integrate self-care into your life in a way that best meets your needs.

This is a how-to book, and at the same time, it's much more than that. You'll find a variety of self-care practices you can put to use, as well as the key ingredients that will help you make self-care into a way of life, rather than just a routine.

Self-care is crucial to our experience of our day-to-day lives and to other people's experiences of us. In the first part of this book, we'll explore why self-care is so important, examine the difference between long-term and short-term self-care, and discover different methods with which you can experiment for creating sustainable habits. We'll also discuss how to deal with the dreaded resistance (which, by the way, is very common; most of us deal with this on a daily basis).

We'll cover these foundations first, because this book is about the whole self-care package.

When I began consciously addressing my own self-care, I launched straight into scheming and whipped up a detailed and intensive self-care routine without having a clear understanding of *why* it was so important (except that many people in the personal development world say it's a good idea). I quickly discovered that it's hard to figure out what works best for us without knowing *why* we're engaging in self-care in the first place and what needs we want to address.

If we don't know what we need from our self-care, we cannot meet those needs. Instead, we end up fumbling around, engaging in various activities that might feel very pleasant, but don't quite hit the spot. Alternatively, we start engaging in activities that meet some of our needs but sacrifice others. We might also confuse self-care with pampering, end up feeling unfulfilled, and decide that this whole self-care malarkey is a load of woo-woo nonsense anyway.

As well as knowing the "why" behind our self-care and how we can best meet our needs, we need to *get to know ourselves* in order to make self-care a way of life. We need to be conscious of what's going to get in our way, times when we will most need self-care, which activities fill us to the brim, and which activities are more draining than nurturing. We need to know what our resistance tells us, and how to work with ourselves to build a sustainable self-care practice.

This book will address all the above and more.

You might be approaching this book from one of the following perspectives: Perhaps you already have a self-care routine but want to delve deeper and find out how to make your self-care even more satisfying, meaningful, and life affirming than it already is. Perhaps you're slightly wary of the whole idea of self-care (I know I certainly was), but you also have a sense that something needs to give. You're tired of feeling stressed, stretched, foggy, and disconnected. Or maybe you like the sound of "self-care," but don't know where to start; you can't afford to splash a ton of cash on spa days, and you don't have much time to spend on yourself.

Wherever you're coming from, this book will act as a guide, supporting you in creating the self-care practice that is right for you. Over the following pages, we'll talk about how you can build a toolkit of nourishing self-care activities that will support you, encourage you, and provide you with a solid internal foundation so you can meet the world as the best version of yourself.

Let's get to it.

PART 1

Laying the Foundations

DON'T JUST SURVIVE, LIVE

To be yourself in a world that is constantly trying to make you something else is the greatest accomplishment.

—*Ralph Waldo Emerson*

"How can I:

- Stop watching so much TV?
- Cut down my drinking?
- Stop spending so much money?
- Stop smoking?
- Get fitter?
- Eat more healthily?
- Experience a richer social life?
- Get enough sleep?
- Reduce my busyness?
- Improve my relationships?"

This book will answer all of those questions, and more. By the time you finish reading, you'll have the ideas and resources you need to switch the coping strategies above for behaviors that will help you thrive.

Before we begin, however, let's start with another question:

What does self-care mean to you?

It's a question I have struggled with for many years, only recently realizing that the answer is hard to define in strong, tangible terms. The goalposts move according to how I'm feeling, what's happening in my life, and what needs I want to meet at the time.

My favorite definition of self-care comes from Pauline Salvucci, author of *Self-Care Now!* (Salvucci, 2001.) She defines self-care as: "*the right and responsibility to take care of your physical, emotional, and spiritual well-being.*"

I selected this definition because it includes several key facts about self-care:

- **Self-care involves our physical, emotional, and spiritual needs.** As I mentioned briefly in the introduction, self-care is less about going out and doing things that fall under the category of "pampering," and more about consciously taking steps to meet our needs in these three areas.

- **Self-care is our right.** Another way of phrasing this is: "we all deserve self-care"—even if it doesn't feel that way sometimes. If you experience internal debate around whether or not you deserve self-care, I'll talk more about this in a later chapter, *Resistance*.

- **Self-care is our responsibility.** Yes, that means that no one is going to take care of us—it's down to us and us alone. Although it's not always conscious, many of us yearn for someone to come along and take care of us, to assume a nurturing parent role, and to meet our unmet needs. While we're waiting for that unspecified (and nonexistent) person to come along, we're neglecting our needs. Taking responsibility for our own self-care allows us to enter into mutually beneficial relationships to meet our needs, rather than being dependent on someone else. Like the question around "deserving" self-care, I'll talk more about the white knight fallacy in *Resistance*.

The secret ingredient to real, genuine self-care is very simple, yet many people miss its power.

At its essence, its very core, self-care is about *identifying and meeting your needs*.

Self-care is integral to our relationship with ourselves and our relationship with the outside world. It provides us with a chance to rest, replenish, and re-nourish physically, mentally, and emotionally.

As children, we rely on our parents and caregivers to meet our needs and take care of ourselves. As adults, we are the only people who can meet our own needs, and that's what self-care is all about. When we engage in self-care, we send ourselves the message: "You are worth taking care of."

What are our needs, and why do they matter?

We all have a variety of human needs that range from basics—like food, shelter, safety, and sleep—to existential needs, like self-expression, acceptance, stability, empathy, and to know and to be known. These needs are the driving force behind our decisions and actions, even if we're not conscious of them at the time. These needs have a deep influence on our internal worlds and our external behavior. Therefore, we need to meet these needs if we're going to have the best possible experience of our lives.

Even if we're not consciously aware of our needs (or we are, but we reject them), parts of us will still be working away under the surface, trying to meet them. This is a recipe for disaster. It leads to us doing things, saying things, and feeling things that we just don't understand. It leads to depression, procrastination, and a whole host of other undesirable phenomena. It keeps us stuck in the same patterns over and over again, and it curbs our ability to live to our full potential.

The parts of us that are left trying to meet these unmet needs are entering a tennis game blindfolded. We hear the "thwack" of the ball from our partner and swing wildly, running all over the court in an attempt to guess where that ball has gone. Soon, we're drained, frustrated, and feeling rather helpless; meeting our needs takes energy—even more so when we're trying to do it unconsciously.

To create a meaningful and fulfilling self-care practice, we need to develop our awareness of our unmet needs. When we're unconsciously working to meet one or more needs, either because part of us has rejected them, or because we're disconnected from them altogether, we aren't going to be able to engage in activities that will truly meet those needs.

When we are conscious of our needs, when we accept them, and when we work out what we need to do to meet them directly, we free up that emotional and physical energy. We're back in the tennis game, blindfold off and ready. We're able to hone our skills, play our best game, feel good about our performance and provide a satisfying experience for our game partner, too.

When we're aware of our needs, we free up a huge amount of headspace. We can live our lives without feeling distracted and weighed down by malaise, emptiness, and that "something's missing" feeling. In a nutshell, we are freer to live the life we want to lead as the best version of ourselves.

This is a vital process, so we're going to get right into it. The next few chapters start by focusing on the key obstacles to self-care and your most important unmet needs.

2

OBSTACLES TO SELF-CARE

There is no need to go to India or anywhere else to find peace. You will find that deep place of silence right in your room, your garden or even your bathtub.

—Elisabeth Kubler-Ross

Many people have a common misconception that self-care is something you do when you have a certain lifestyle, with a certain amount of income, and a certain amount of time to spare. The fact is; that's just not true.

Self-care is healthcare.

Just as we might go see doctors and dentists, we need to take care of our existential needs too. We are in the best position to be the best version of ourselves, fulfill our dreams, live our potential, have our best relationships, do our best work, and most importantly, enjoy life when we have taken care of our needs.

In fact, we are *only* able to be the best version of ourselves, fulfill our dreams, live our potential, have our best relationships, and do our best work when we have taken care of our needs.

This reality runs counter to the popular view that it's selfish to put ourselves first. Many of us struggle with feeling like we haven't yet achieved enough, been enough, earned enough, or sacrificed enough to be worthy of self-care. This was the place I started from when I began taking my self-care seriously. It took me a long time to understand that this was a chicken-egg situation: I was reluctant to engage in self-care and take time to focus on meeting my needs in a healthy and sustainable way until I felt I was worthy of doing so, but I didn't necessarily feel like I was worthy of doing so until I started engaging in self-care and meeting my needs in a healthy and sustainable way.

This Catch-22 situation is partly due to our cultural fanaticism about altruism, putting others first, and the virtue of hard work. Many of us are raised to believe that we only deserve a day off if we've been working ourselves to the bone. Once this belief becomes embedded in our self-concept, it's hard to shift. I used to view one day off in four months as an achievement, not as a sign that something was severely wrong with the fun quotient in my life. I rarely stopped working when I got sick, and I took pride in pushing myself as far as I could go. I felt effective, efficient, and terribly unhappy. I've found that I need to be constantly vigilant of how I approach the balance between "work" and "leisure" activities in my life; otherwise this balance will inevitably tip in favor of the "work" side.

With the gift of hindsight, I can look back and see that my desire to be constantly working and constantly busy came from a need to feel worthy. In addition, I had a sense that if I just lived my life as myself, not "Hannah, who does all of these things and does them well," then I wouldn't be enough.

We all have many needs that fit under the overarching category of "worthiness." The constant struggle to meet these needs is one I've seen many times over in people who aren't happy with the way their life is playing out, yet aren't aware that it is internal shifts, not external changes, that will lead to the change they are seeking. As I'll talk about in the next chapter, being busy is a great coping strategy and one of the biggest emotional barriers to self-care. For now, I want to move the focus to two of the biggest practical (and, secondarily, emotional) barriers to self-care: *money* and *time*.

Money

Most of us have a complicated relationship with money.

Money has come to represent so much in our culture that many of us equate our financial worth with our personal worth. When this happens, we feel worth more as a person when we have, or are earning, more money; and worth less as a person when we have, or are earning, less money. These feelings of having more or less value greatly impact our behavior and our feelings around whether we are worthy of self-care. When we equate our financial worth with our self-worth, we might give ourselves permission to engage in self-care only when things are going "well" financially. Equally, financial challenges can leave us feeling stressed, isolated, and lacking in some way.

Of course, there are many reasons why we might struggle to accept our current finances: maybe we're under-earning; perhaps we're unconscious about where our money goes every month; maybe we're shouldering a lot of debt, perhaps we have an addictive or compulsive behavior that has a negative impact on our finances; or maybe we've recently gone through a life transition—such as divorce, redundancy or death—that has changed our financial situation. These things aren't necessarily a reflection of us as people; however, they can feel that way. We encounter practical situations, or we develop certain behavioral and spending patterns, that not only shake our sense of security and stability, but also our sense of worthiness.

The link between financial worth and self-worth won't be true for absolutely everyone. However, money and finances are complex topics, and many of us aren't even aware how much emotional investment we have in them. This connection is not only something I've struggled with myself, but also an issue I've come across repeatedly when listening to other people's experiences. It feels important to highlight the connection between the two types of worth here, as well as the possible connection between our financial situation and our level of self-care. After all, the awarer we are of these connections, the less unconscious power they have over us.

Time

"I don't have time to dedicate to self-care" is another common reason people feel excluded from the club. I want to start with a home truth. Emotion and tone can be difficult to convey through writing, so please know that I offer the following words with compassion, not judgment:

It's not a question of enough time; it's a question of priorities.

No doubt your day is filled with errands, tasks, and activities that feel important. I want you to ask yourself:

- What makes them more important than self-care?

Now, have a think about the following:

- How would your ability to handle the load on your plate improve if you were operating at your most efficient, switched on, motivated, and energized?

When we're cash poor, time poor, or a combination of both, we might not feel like we have the time or resources to engage in self-care; however, I have a different perspective:

Far from being a time when we don't deserve self-care, this is the time when we *most need* self-care.

The times when we feel like we least deserve self-care are the times when it will be most useful to us.

Therefore, the times when we think we least deserve self-care are the times when it will be most helpful to show ourselves care.

Although they are hard to avoid sometimes, I hesitate to use the words "need," "should," or "must" in relation to self-care. Often these words carry a sense of obligation and feed our inner shame gremlins (to borrow a term from researcher and writer Dr. Brené Brown). I'm very aware of the fine line between making suggestions and saying that you, as the reader, "should" be doing or "need" to do XYZ for this reason. This distinction is important, so it's something I discuss in more detail in a later chapter, *Self-care and Shame*.

The truth about self-care, and how to "do it"

Our society perpetuates the pervasive and influential story that self-care revolves around external activities and actions (going to a spa, buying a new mud mask, etc.). According to popular belief, the equation goes:

Self-care = external factors influencing our internal feelings.

This is a myth.

Eighty to ninety percent of self-care is an inside job.

This means that most of our self-care revolves around our *internal processes*. It's about how we interact with ourselves, how we deal with our internal conflicts, how we process information from external circumstances, and how our history affects the way we go about this.

When we try to "do" self-care by flitting from external activity to external activity, we're neglecting to pay attention to our unmet underlying needs. Most importantly, we're neglecting to *set an intention* for what we want to get out of our self-care.

Self-care is about knowing which needs we want to fulfil, knowing how we want to feel, and seeking out nourishing and nurturing activities that will meet those needs and generate those feelings.

As much as we might hear about the vegan meditation yoga countryside retreats (and as great as they might sound), it's not the vegan meditation yoga countryside retreat that we specifically need right now. What we're yearning for when we desire something like that are the *feelings it creates in us*.

With this in mind, it's important to distinguish between self-care and self-indulgence, or pampering. Self-care is about starting with an unmet need or desired feeling. Self-indulgence is about feeling good right here, right now, regardless of whether we're meeting our underlying long-term needs. Many activities that conventionally file under the label "self-care" (spa days, massages—except to relieve aches, pains, and tension—manicures, makeovers, and so on) are actually self-indulgence. There's nothing wrong with self-indulgence (who doesn't like to feel good?), but these activities alone are not necessarily going to help us meet our unmet needs. In this way, self-indulgence can become similar to coping strategies (more on these in the next chapter) and often involves meeting one or more of our needs at the expense of one or more of our other needs. True self-care is about identifying and taking steps to meet our needs without compromising other needs.

Now that we've noted the difference between self-care and self-indulgence, we can bust the no-time and no-money myths for good:

Self-care is about your relationship with yourself. Consequently, the amount of money in your bank account, or the amount of time in your weekly schedule, has nothing to do with your levels of self-care.

As you'll see from the list of suggestions coming up, you can choose from a variety of self-care activities that don't require massive amounts of time or money. Whatever you choose to include in your self-care practice, the effects of your self-care will be hit or miss if you don't ask two questions.

For self-care with maximum effectiveness, that impacts you right where you need it to, consider:

- *What do I want to get out of my self-care?* (In other words, what is my intention?)

- *How do I want to feel having engaged in this self-care practice?*

Simple questions, but taking the time to consider them will boost your self-care to a whole new level.

Before we continue...

We're going to talk about the crucial difference between coping strategies and self-care in the next chapter but, before we move on, I want to mention another common self-care mistake that has tripped me up in the past and requires vigilance.

As I mentioned, self-indulgence doesn't always fill the function of self-care because when we indulge, we risk meeting one or more of our needs *at the expense of one or more of our other needs*. When we engage in an act of self-care, it's important to make sure that we're not doing this; otherwise it's not really self-care at all. For example, if we have the need for sleep and the need for connection, staying up until 2am talking with friends will meet the need for connection, but that's going to be at the expense of our need for sleep.

In the context of self-care, this is especially important when it comes to the two hot topics above: *money* and *time*. We're so used to thinking about self-care as something that requires a lot of time and money that we don't recognize that self-care is a totally separate entity.

Money in particular can provoke all kinds of complicated emotional and physical feelings. At two extreme ends of the scale, a proportion of people believe it is wrong to spend money on themselves, while, at the other end, a proportion of people believe that spending money on themselves will make them feel better. Equally, if you're feeling pushed and pulled in many directions time-wise, you want whatever self-care activities you engage in to be respectful and allowing of that, not to deepen your stress.

When we try to create a self-care practice containing activities that conflict with certain needs, those needs will strike back. If we're meeting some needs at the expense of others, those unmet needs will find a way to get themselves heard. More often than not, this will cost you your self-care practice. Your unmet needs will show up as internal conflict, resistance, self-criticism, and a range of other possible (equally unpleasant) manifestations. Even if you manage to maintain your self-care practice, it's not self-care if it's provoking self-attack.

Being aware of, and negotiating between, these conflicting needs can be challenging and often comes down to a trial and error process. I've attempted to include a range of suggestions in this book that you can tailor in such a way as to meet your unmet needs without sacrificing other needs at the same time. When it comes to choosing your self-care practices, think first about whether a particular practice will cause a conflict in needs and, if so, how you can negotiate that with yourself or adapt the suggestion so that it better meets your needs as a whole.

3

COPING STRATEGIES AND SHADOW COMFORTS

It is only possible to live happily ever after on a day to day basis.

—Margaret Bonnano

Spoiler alert: this is the most important chapter of the book. Even if you stop reading after this section and don't take anything else away from our time together, I hope you will think carefully about what we're about to discuss and how it might impact your own self-care.

The number one self-care mistake that many people (myself included) make is confusing *self-care and coping strategies* (or, as writer and coach Jennifer Louden calls them, *shadow comforts*).

Here, we're going to talk about the difference between these two types of activities. This can be a tricky topic because we all have coping strategies that deep down we know are coping strategies (even if we don't call them by the same name), and we'd rather not give them up. As we're about to explore, coping strategies seem very similar to self-care on the surface—after all, the point of coping strategies is that they help us *cope*—but underneath they are very, very different.

Let's start at the beginning.

As we grow, gain life experiences, and start to learn where our hot buttons are (where we need the most care and compassion, what situations are stressful to us, and which needs are most important), we develop a set of responses that fall into one of two categories:

- Coping strategies

- Self-Care

The difference between them is simple: *coping strategies* are behaviors we use to relieve a sense of pain or discomfort in the short-term but don't serve our well-being in the long-term. These might include behaviors like smoking, drinking, drugs, eating for comfort, and so on. These coping strategies have a similar benefit to the "short-term self-care" practices we're going to talk about in the next chapter (except they also come with many drawbacks). They are the equivalent of slapping a Band-Aid on a wound that really needs stitches; they might provide some short-term relief, but in the long run they possibly do more harm than good.

By *self-care*, I mean behaviors that serve our emotional and physical health over the short-term and the long-term. These include practices like journaling, eating nourishing, healthy food, learning to sit with our emotions rather than react to them, and so on.

So if we can engage in short-term self-care practices, why do we develop coping strategies in the first place?

How do coping strategies develop?

There are many potential answers to this question, and I'm going to discuss two in brief here.

First, our self-care methods might not give us the same immediate short-term release from a feeling of pain or discomfort that some coping strategies will. Many coping strategies involve activities that produce chemical changes in our bodies, such as a rush of adrenaline, or the addition of external stimulants or depressants like nicotine, sugar, or alcohol.

Furthermore, we are more likely to turn to coping strategies to deal with challenging or uncomfortable feelings or situations if that was how we saw other people responding to these kinds of feelings or situations as children. When we grow up with parents or caregivers who rely on substances or compulsive behaviors to deal with their emotions, we're far more likely to use coping mechanisms ourselves as adults. This is because that particular method of coping with stressful or difficult events is the one that's been modeled for us (over, for example, sitting down to talk about how we're feeling). Although we might know on a logical level that doing these things isn't good for us in the long-term, we don't have a template for what it looks like to deal with emotions in a healthy and productive way.

When you look at their origins and their purpose, you can see that self-care and coping strategies are two very different entities.

What does the difference between self-care and coping strategies look like?

Let's imagine we're faced with a common stressful situation. We might be working to several deadlines and running late on all of them, we might be facing financial or job insecurity, or we might be having trouble with one or more personal relationships.

In these kinds of situations, dealing with our stress using coping strategies might include:

- Dissociating through watching TV (even programs or channels we don't enjoy)
- Drinking excessively or relying on a drink to "take the edge off" each day
- Drinking excessive amounts of caffeine to "keep going"
- Using recreational drugs
- Smoking
- Spending money (or living extremely frugally) to feel "better"
- Comfort eating or limiting our food intake
- Being "busy" and taking on too many commitments
- Repeatedly getting into and spending time on unhealthy relationships
- Avoiding social situations
- Self-punishment or self-harm
- Acting out on other people (yelling, intimidation, verbal or physical abuse)

Examples of self-care might include:

- Reaching out to talk to someone about how we're feeling and talking to a professional, if appropriate
- Putting boundaries around our time
- Setting aside time to exercise
- Using meditation and other relaxation techniques
- Spending time with close friends and family
- Engaging in a creative activity, like writing or art
- Finding a constructive outlet for intense or overwhelming emotions, such as writing in a journal or taking the space and time to cry
- Ensuring that whatever is happening, we're giving ourselves time to get enough sleep
- Reducing our caffeine and alcohol intake
- Keeping our diets clean and healthy

As I've already mentioned in previous chapters, "self-care"-type reactions focus on meeting the unmet needs we might have in the above situations. When we rely on coping strategies to get through the day, we are not truly meeting our underlying needs and this will show in our daily lives.

How to tell the difference between self-care and coping strategies in your life

Here is a set of questions you can ask yourself to evaluate whether an activity counts as self-care or coping strategy:

1. *What need am I trying to meet with this activity?*

2. *Does it involve some kind of potentially addictive substance?*

3. *Will I regret it afterwards?*

4. *What is the true intention behind this activity? (Am I looking to escape what's currently happening in my life, or am I looking to process it? Do I want to engage with this particular activity to numb my emotions and get rid of my discomfort, or do I want to take care of the need underneath?)*

5. *What will the effects of this activity be if I continue engaging in it over the long-term? Will they be helpful or harmful?*

6. *What does my gut tell me about this activity? Is there a part of me that is saying this is not what I need right now?*

How to switch from coping to caring

The most effective way I've found to switch from coping strategies to self-care is to replace one with the other, rather than to give up or quit coping strategies. As you'll see in parts three, four, and five, I've organized the self-care suggestions in this book according to which needs they meet. The most effective way to be the best version of yourself is to identify which coping mechanisms you're using, identify which needs we're trying to meet through using these mechanisms, and replace the coping mechanisms with genuine self-care activities that will truly meet that need, not just slap a Band-Aid on it.

We'll be sticking with this switch throughout the rest of the book and exploring some of the coping strategies you're using right now in a few chapters' time. For now, here is a brief step-by-step overview of how the transition works:

1. Identify the coping mechanisms you are currently using (the purpose of this isn't to judge, only to notice what's happening in your life right now).

2. Identify the needs underneath. You might find the Needs Inventory on the Nonviolent Communication Website helpful for this.

3. Match the needs to a self-care activity that is likely to meet them.

4. Rinse and repeat.

It sounds simple (and it is), but this is where self-knowledge is crucial and gaining that self-knowledge takes time. To switch from coping to caring, you need to be willing to look at reality as it is right now, how you're spending your time, what you're needing, and how you can meet those needs. Coping can be a comfortable and familiar place to be in the short-term, so you also need to be willing to be uncomfortable for a while. It won't be easy; you might be thinking that this is going somewhere you hadn't bargained for. As someone who has been there, I can put my hand on my heart and tell you that the rewards of doing the work, examining the hard stuff and making that switch are more than worth it.

4

LONG-TERM VERSUS SHORT-TERM SELF-CARE

"Nourishing yourself in a way that helps you blossom in the direction you want to go is attainable, and you are worth the effort."

—Deborah Day

In this chapter, I want to talk about the difference between long-term and short-term self-care. As we saw from the definition of self-care in the second chapter, it is *"the right and responsibility to take care of your physical, emotional, and spiritual well-being."* In other words, self-care encompasses a wide range of activities, not all of which we'd necessarily describe as pleasant...

On my own self-care journey, it quickly became clear to me that there were two distinct types of self-care. There are the self-care activities that we look forward to, that feel special, provide immediate rewards, and are ultimately a positive experience. General resistance to self-care aside (which we'll talk about later), these are the activities that are "easy." When offered the opportunity to take part in them, our immediate response is usually "Yes please!" and, when we have them booked or scheduled, we usually look forward to them beforehand.

Then, you'll also come across a completely different type of self-care activity. These are the self-care activities that provoke internal conflict and result in general feet dragging and a sense of "Do I really *have* to?" These are activities we know are ultimately good for us, yet each time we want to undertake them, first we have to muster up steely internal willpower and scale the craggy peaks of Mount Resistance.

Activities in both these categories fall under the banner of "self-care," yet in the moment they feel very, very different.

We need to be aware of the difference between these two activities because, if we're not, we risk selecting one type of self-care (the "easy" type) and neglecting the other. It's not in our best interests to engage in self-care activities that meet some of our needs at the expense of others, and it's also not in our best interests just to engage in "easy" self-care activities and avoid those that don't provide much immediate gratification. Both types of activities are absolutely crucial to our physical and mental health, as we'll see over the next few pages.

Long-term self-care

I use the phrase *long-term self-care* to describe activities that might not be that pleasant in the moment, but contribute to our health, well-being, and longevity over a period of many weeks, months, or years. This category includes activities like exercising, going to the dentist, getting vaccinations, visiting a chiropractor, and other unsavory activities that require a certain determination and willpower to undertake (and that we'd probably avoid if we had the choice).

These activities are an important part of self-care. Along with the suggestions I talk about later, they are the *foundations* of our self-care practice. They're also some of the hardest self-care habits to maintain because most of them don't provide much of a short-term payoff (our immediate experience might even be negative). When we start spending 20 minutes on a treadmill a few times per week, it can take weeks or months before we notice any difference in our fitness. When we undergo dentistry work, we can end up in more pain initially, only to experience the benefits several weeks later.

When we are working with constraints on our budget and/or time, it's even easier to delay these activities, especially when they cost money or take precious hours out of our day. The financial and time commitment involved adds another excuse to the resistance arsenal—and a convincing one at that.

What is really underlying the resistance is (understandably) the *discomfort* involved in each situation. Injections, drilling, extractions, medical examinations, exercise—in the moment, all these things can feel downright unpleasant. Yet they are so important for our long-term health and quality of life.

To reiterate what I wrote earlier, these uncomfortable-in-the-short-term-but-necessary-in-the-long-term kind of activities form the *foundations* of our self-care practice. Once we're aware that these activities are ultimately in our best interests and that our resistance arises from the discomfort involved, we're in a much better position to make a conscious decision to put our well-being first, over and above our short-term comfort.

Short-term self-care

Now that we've talked about the hard part, let's look at a more pleasant form of self-care: what I call *short-term self-care*. Short-term self-care involves actions and activities that provide us with immediate gratification and gain. This involves activities like meditation (although this can also fall into the long-term self-care category too), a massage, relaxation techniques, and other activities that help us reconnect with ourselves and our needs in the moment. As you read the suggestions included later in this book, you'll see that the majority of them (with a few key exceptions) involve short-term self-care.

Earlier in this chapter, I referred to these activities as "easy," but I also want to acknowledge that this isn't always the case. Just as many long-term self-care activities provoke discomfort-related resistance in the moment, pleasant and enjoyable activities can provoke their own kind of discomfort and resistance too. These activities can be especially challenging to people on a budget or those who have little spare time, as they might seem like superfluous luxuries that aren't necessary. For some of the activities that might be true—remember that our self-care shouldn't be meeting some of our needs at the expense of others.

Short-term self-care practices are the layers that build on your long-term self-care activities. They are the practices you can use to revitalize your self-care when all the foundations are in place. And the foundations *must* be in place for you to get the most benefit from these practices. Adequate food, sleep, and health will transform the way you experience these self-care practices and yourself.

5

HOW TO CREATE SUSTAINABLE HABITS

If you want to know what your experiences were like in the past, examine your body now. If you want to know what your body will look like in the future, examine your experiences now.

—Ancient Proverb

I don't know about you, but "habit" is a word that fills me with a sense of dread. As someone who has repeatedly experienced the challenges inherent in creating "healthy" habits (and the ease with which "unhealthy" habits seem to spring up out of nowhere), habits have historically felt like one of the universe's greatest mysteries.

As unromantic as it sounds, creating a sustainable practice out of self-care is the first step to integrating self-care into our lifestyle. With that in mind, I want to share a selection of ideas that I've found helpful when it comes to my own healthy habit formation.

Creating sustainable habits is a challenge we all face at one point or another. The subject of much academic, scientific, and psychological discussion, it's an existential irony that we usually find it easy to create habits involving things that are bad for us (TV watching, sugar, alcohol, cigarettes, comfort eating) and teeth-grittingly hard to create habits involving activities that are good for our health.

So what can we do to start formulating "good" habits? I wish there was a simple answer to that question! Several different aspects of our personality, lifestyle, and psyche influence the way we develop habits, so the answer is likely to be highly personal to individuals. Here, I want to share a few tips that I've found helpful in my own experiences with building habits:

1. Define the emotional need behind the habit
2. Set realistic goals
3. Build habits one at a time
4. Get some outside help

1. Define the emotional need behind the habit

Part of the reason we develop habits is to meet our *emotional needs*. Many of the behaviors we chalk up as "bad habits" are designed to fulfill some sort of emotional need—and fulfill it quickly. In other words, many of the "bad habits" we develop are coping mechanisms.

You'll remember from the previous chapter, *Long Term Versus Short Term Self-Care*, that one of the potential barriers to long-term self-care is that there are very few activities in this category that show immediate results, or even provide immediate pleasure. Therefore, when it comes to fulfilling emotional needs, healthy habits already have a black mark against them, as deep down the parts of us that have these emotional needs know that it's going to take weeks, even months, to meet our emotional needs through those habits. The unhealthy habits, on the other hand, are winners in this sense. With the vast majority of these habits, the quick-fix relief is what we feel almost immediately, (and any regret or self-recrimination we might feel comes later).

These habits put a Band-Aid over the emotional need in the moment., but they don't actually meet the need itself. Instead of bringing us closer to meeting our needs, this quick fix distracts us from taking action that would better meet our needs in the long term.

Let's take a stereotypical example of Band-Aiding needs:

Boy breaks up with girl, girl goes home, puts on soppy movie and, over the course of the evening, proceeds to down a bottle of wine, accompanied by a box of chocolates and/or Ben and Jerry's Cookie Dough ice cream.

The possible emotional needs she might be trying to meet include a need for connection, reassurance, comfort, and support. A movie, bottle of wine, chocolate, and ice cream aren't actually going to give her those things. But they do provide distraction (movie) an anxiety-relieving depressant (wine), and a sugar rush (chocolate or Ben and Jerry's). Girl will wake up tomorrow and still have unmet emotional needs (plus a hangover and Ben and Jerry's regret). When her feelings are too uncomfortable to handle in the moment, however, all those things serve to put a Band-Aid over them.

So, we find it easier to create habits when they fulfil a need. There's no point in doing something just because we heard it was good for us. Unless we can recognize a tangible benefit and make that benefit conscious, we will be locked in a perpetual struggle against ourselves as we try to transform a particular action into a habit.

As you go through the following sections of this book and read each self-care idea, think about the following question:

"How could this suggestion meet one or more of my needs?"

Simply recognizing that will bring you one step closer to forming a sustainable self-care practice.

2. Set realistic goals

The biggest killer of new habits is *ambition*. Not ambition to make something a habit, but the kind of self-sabotaging ambition that provokes us into setting unrealistic goals for ourselves.

Perhaps this situation sounds familiar:

You start a new exercise routine and decide that instead of easing in, you're going to start by hitting it hard. After all, if you're going to do it, you might as well do it properly, right?

So let's say you decide to go running three times per week, fill in with yoga another two days, and then have two rest days. You plan an exercise program for the next three months, stick it up on your wall, and start ticking off the days you complete.

After about a week, the schedule starts to feel a little overwhelming in amongst your other daily commitments. You begin to resent it. Perhaps you set yourself fitness goals, too (e.g., to run in a 10 km race this summer), and are struggling to keep up with them. You're not sure this is such a great idea anymore. Either way, you haven't seen any of the positive effects you were hoping to see yet.

Your next running day comes around, and it's raining. Already demotivated, it's not hard to justify skipping a day. But then you also skip the next day, then the next, and before you know it, you're a week behind on your schedule and have fallen off the wagon. Frustrated (and maybe ashamed) at having done so, you call it quits, declaring you're just too busy to start a new exercise routine right now.

Most of us have experienced the above at least a few times (or in my case, at least 20) in different contexts. Whether it's exercise, diet, a routine, a hobby, or anything else that's new, if you can identify with having an "all or nothing" approach, it can be hard to embody the flexibility you need to have to create new habits.

Start low and set realistic goals you *know* you can achieve. Make it easy for yourself. If you have a vocal inner taskmaster, as I do, this can be a real challenge, but it is doable. Habit building is not the same as an endurance test where you have to push yourself to the limit from day one. It's about making it easy and enjoyable enough to want to come back on day two, three, four, and beyond.

For example, instead of setting up a running schedule dictating that you must run three times a week on Monday, Wednesday, and Friday between the hours of 7.30am and 8.15am, start by saying, "I'm going to go running at least once per week. If I want to go running more, I can, but when I've done my one minimum, that's my commitment fulfilled." Do what you need to do to make it official: write it on a Post-It, stick it on your wall, or create a contract with yourself. Whatever you choose to do, make it a commitment, without letting your inner taskmaster up the stakes behind your back.

There is a difference between self-discipline and self-flagellation. One is the key to forming new habits; the other is kryptonite.

Setting these low expectations and goals removes this self-sabotaging frustration and self-recrimination we experience when we don't hit our self-imposed targets. It's easy to meet our goal and easy to exceed it, too. Once we feel comfortable with that goal, we can step it up as much as we want. What's important though is that our goals are *realistic* and, in the long term, involve activities that we actually want to be doing.

3. Build habits one at a time

The next concept that will help make self-care habit-forming easier is to focus on one habit at a time and prioritize that single goal for as long as it takes to develop a habit.

For example, you feel you aren't getting as much sleep as you need to feel well-rested, and you want to start going to bed earlier during the week. To do this, you could set a specific time and make going to bed at that time a priority for the next couple of weeks or months (or as long as it takes for that new time to become part of your routine). When it comes to your weekday evenings, prioritize going to bed early over everything else. Plan your evening around going to bed early, instead of planning your bedtime around everything else you're doing that night.

Focusing and prioritizing are not sexy, but they are a great way of making stuff we want to happen, happen.

4. Get some outside help

Make forming new habits easy. Set reminders, task alerts; do whatever you need to do to help yourself create the habits you want.

I know that I feel more alive and more connected to myself when I exercise, journal, and meditate, yet I often find myself distracted by other activities in my life. One of the most successful ways I've found to combat that is to use technology. I have a meditation app on my phone that sends me a daily reminder. I've listed 750 words (journaling), exercise, and meditation as recurring to-dos in my task manager software. The journaling software I use also sends me daily reminder emails. Even with all of this, I still sometimes get caught up in other things and forget to do one or more of these activities!

Do what you need to do to give yourself the best chance of honoring your commitment to yourself. The more you are able to do this, the easier it will become.

Advice from others

You can find much conflicting advice on forming healthy habits, and what works for one person isn't necessarily going to work for another. The two resources below provide different perspectives around the practices and challenges involved in forming habits. I've included these so that you can start to think about how you can best approach your habits.

Leo Babauta, Zen Habits

The first is a blog post by Leo Babauta, who writes at zenhabits.net. In January 2013, he wrote about discomfort—namely, that if we can learn to live with discomfort, we can pretty much master **anything**. Busting procrastination, developing a new exercise regime, changing our habits, daily meditation, learning a new skill, de-junkifying our house, dealing with paperwork, striking out, trying new experiences, and seeking new adventures—all these things are within our grasp if we can learn to live with discomfort.

Here is his advice:

"Mastering Discomfort

The way to master discomfort is to do it comfortably. That might sound contradictory, but it's not. If you are afraid of discomfort, and you try to beat discomfort with a really grueling activity, you will probably give up and fail, and go back to comfort.

So do it in small doses.

1. **Pick something that's not hard.** Take meditation as an example. It's not really that hard — you just sit down and pay attention to your body and breath, in the present moment. You don't have to empty your mind (just notice your thoughts), you don't have to chant anything weird, you just sit and pay attention. If you don't like meditation, try a new healthy food, like kale or raw almonds or quinoa. Or a fairly easy exercise if you're sedentary, like walking or jogging.
2. **Just do a little.** You don't have to start by doing 30 minutes of something you're not used to doing. Just do a few minutes. Just start.
3. **Push out of your comfort zone, a little.** My friend and Zen priest Susan O'Connell has a favorite meditation instruction that you can use for any activity actually: when you're meditating and you feel like getting up, don't; then when you feel the urge to get up a second time, don't; and when you feel the urge to get up a third time, then get up. So you sit through the urge, the discomfort, twice before finally giving in the third time. This is a nice balance, so that you're pushing your comfort zone a little. You can do this in exercise and many other activities — push a little.
4. **Watch the discomfort.** Watch yourself as you get a bit uncomfortable — are you starting to complain (internally)? Are you looking for ways to avoid it? Where do you turn to? What happens if you stay with it, and don't do anything?
5. **Smile.** This is not trivial advice. If you can smile while being uncomfortable, you can learn to be happy with discomfort, with practice. When I did the Goruck Challenge in 2011, it was 13 hours of discomfort — raw and bloody knees, sand in my shoes as I hiked and ran with 60+ pounds on my back, carrying teammates and logs, doing pushups and crabwalks and other exercises, needing the bathroom and being tired and hungry and cold. And yet, I practiced something simple: I tried to maintain a smile through all this discomfort. It's an important practice.

Repeat this practice daily. It will be strange, perhaps difficult, at first, but soon your comfort zone will expand. If you practice it enough, with different activities, your comfort zone will expand to include discomfort. And then you can master the universe."

Tiny Habits

Another useful framework for developing habits comes from a concept called "Tiny Habits" (you can find details of this on the Resources page for this book: www.becomingwhoyouare.net/fctt-resources).

Here's how it works:

The project is a weeklong e-course run by Dr. BJ Fogg, a Stanford University Professor. It uses context and baby steps to encourage participants to create new habits.

When you sign up, you choose three habits you want to practice during the week ahead. These have to match specific criteria (for example, they should take 30 seconds or less). You then attach them to an "anchor"—something you already do at least once a day, like using the bathroom or brushing your teeth.

During your Tiny Habits week, you follow the daily anchor behavior with your tiny habit. By the end of the week, the two behaviors become associated, and the tiny habit becomes a proper habit.

For example, if I decided to do three sit-ups after I send an email, it means I do 30 sit-ups on a day when I send 10 emails, 60 on a day I send 20, and so on. I'm not doing all the sit-ups at once, just three at a time after I send an email, but the number accumulates through the day. It doesn't take much time, and the aim is to integrate the habit as a natural part of your day.

At the time of writing, the program is free and open to anyone. With the "Tiny Habits" structure, you ditch the idea that a new practice needs to be a huge commitment, or that it needs to be done all in one go. Instead, you focus on remembering to do small, repetitive actions whenever you do your "anchor" task.

So there are six ideas to ponder. You might already have thoughts about which of these suggestions and approaches could work for you; you might still be feeling your way through the idea of forming habits. Reflect on what you've read in this chapter as you continue, and consider how you can transition self-care from a low-priority action into a habit.

6

RESISTANCE

The only person who can pull me down is myself, and I'm not going to let myself pull me down anymore.

—C. Joybell C.

At some point on your journey into self-care, you will experience the one thing that is most likely to get in your way: resistance.

Resistance appears in two forms. It can be a sign that we're engaged in something that isn't meeting our needs. It can also be a sign that we are involved in something that *does* meet our needs, but jars with internal beliefs and self-concepts.

In this chapter, we're going to focus on the second category of resistance, as this is the kind of resistance that usually shows up when we're engaging in activities that are good for us.

This is the resistance that appears when we know we really should go to the gym, make that dentist appointment, or say "no" to a particular commitment that isn't serving us. Resistance is not fun, mainly because it creates an internal backlash. Some parts of our internal dialogue focus on why we should do the activity in question, other parts of our internal dialogue focus on why we shouldn't, and there's no easy resolution in sight.

Like many things that are good for us, engaging in a regular self-care practice can provoke feelings of resistance. This resistance has two possible causes:

- Valid obstacles and barriers to self-care

- Ourselves

We're going to talk more about valid obstacles and barriers to self-care in *Things As They Are: Part 1*. In the meantime, here is a selection of questions inspired by self-care maven Jennifer Louden that provides a starting point for thinking about any practical issues:

What circumstances, commitments, relationships, obligations, or other things stop me from relaxing and engaging in self-care?

Over the course of the next week, notice the barriers that arise. You don't necessarily have to take action on them at this stage: this first step is about noticing them.

What are the signs that I haven't been engaging in self-care?

Over the course of the coming week, start noticing what happens when you don't engage in the self-care you need. How do you feel? What physical and emotional symptoms do you start to notice? What behavior patterns manifest? Start collecting these signs into a list. Initially you will notice them in retrospect, after they occur. The more you pay attention to them, the better equipped you'll be to move that awareness from the past into the present moment and recognize them as they're happening.

Dealing with resistance from within

Valid obstacles and barriers to self-care, for the most part, are simpler to overcome than the second piece of the resistance puzzle: ourselves.

Our beliefs around self-care, our attempts to replicate others' self-care advice in a way that doesn't work for us, or making our self-care a casualty of other, deeper beliefs (for example, a struggle to feel worthy), are just a few of the internal patterns that can lead to resistance.

The topic of our inner resistance to self-care could fill a book in itself; however, I'm going to talk about a few key self-made barriers that could be standing in your way:

1. The idea the we "deserve" self-care
2. Self-care is inconsistent with our conditioned beliefs
3. Self-care feels like another obligation
4. White knight syndrome
5. Social and cultural conditioning

1. The idea that we "deserve" self-care

While I was working on my own self-care practice, and then researching this book, often I ran into talk about "deserving" self-care—namely, the idea that "everyone deserves it."

For a long time, I tried to buy into this belief: I wanted to think that everybody deserved self-care. It wasn't something you had to work to deserve, jump through certain hoops to deserve, or be a certain kind of person to deserve; it was just something that *everyone* deserved.

In fact, I really battled with myself, trying to persuade myself that this was the case. Some parts of me were totally on board with the idea that everyone deserves self-care, and others weren't so sure. Despite really *wanting* to believe everyone deserves self-care, the not-so-sure parts persisted.

These parts kept bargaining. They kept trying to make deals, for example I could only really justify taking the whole evening off if I'd finished everything on my task list, I could only really justify doing yoga at lunchtime if I worked late or I could only really justify buying myself something I needed if I could look back and say I had earned it (literally) by working as hard as possible that week.

For a long time, I tried to tell those parts they were wrong—that I deserved these things regardless of how hard I worked. Then I realized that, actually, these parts have a point. I don't "deserve" self-care at all.

The definition of deserved is "to merit, be qualified for, or have a claim to (reward, assistance, punishment, etc.) because of actions, qualities, or situations" (dictionary.com).

It doesn't make sense to talk about whether we deserve self-care, just as it makes no sense to talk about whether we deserve sleep, food, a roof over our heads, exercise, or any of the basic needs that we have to meet to keep ourselves ticking over.

It's not about deserving, it's about *priorities*.

The change in my perception around priorities came after reading how technologist Gwen Bell defines her priorities:

"I put my health first, the people I love second, and the work third."

Simple, right? There's nothing about deserving, earning, claiming, or qualifying for anything, just clear and simple *priorities*.

One of the major problems with the idea that we deserve self-care is that it leaves those of us who are more susceptible to self-criticism feeling like we *don't* deserve self-care. My own internal voices kept telling me that I had to work to deserve things that counted as self-care because I was still thinking about self-care within the framework of deserving—and ultimately, earning—it. Even in the positive (i.e., everyone deserves it), the word "deserve" has cause-and-effect connotations that it can be challenging, if not impossible, to escape. Shifting my mindset from "deserving," taking the moral element out of it, and realizing that it is a simple matter of priorities helped me overcome this internal barrier to self-care.

Self-care is healthcare: mental, physical, and emotional.

When we remove "deserving"—and all the guilt-inducing "do I or don't I" uncertainty from the equation of self-care—we can see it as it really is:

An integral, necessary part of being *alive*.

2. Self-care is inconsistent with our conditioned beliefs

Most of us know on a logical level that self-care is "good." It's something that is healthy, functional, and helpful for our physical and emotional health. In practice, however, our relationship with self-care is a lot more complex—because our feelings about ourselves are complex.

In an ideal world, we would all be raised to want to nourish ourselves, to take care of ourselves, and to do what's best for our bodies and minds. As babies, this is exactly what we do: we might not have the nuanced communication skills we enjoy as adults, but we sure know how to communicate when we're hungry, hot, cold, happy, tired, and a range of different states and emotions. In other words, we know how to communicate our *needs*.

As we grow up, though, we're conditioned by our society and those around us to deny our needs. We're taught to put other people first, criticized in a way that damages our sense of self-worth, or raised with various conditions of worth, for example, that we are only worthy of love and acceptance if we work hard and achieve. If we asked our parents now whether they loved us unconditionally, most would say "Of course!" yet that doesn't change the fact that most, if not all, of us received *underlying messages* based on our parents' and authority figures' own core beliefs, about what was acceptable, what was unacceptable, and what resulted in approval and love.

One of the results of these conditions is that we start to feel uncomfortable spending time and money taking care of number one. Just as we might have received the message that our parents' love and affection was conditional as children, we now set those conditions on our *self*-love and our *self*-care. These messages didn't have to be explicit, in fact most of the time they aren't. They can be as subtle as looks, body language, tone of voice, or overheard conversations. As children, we rely on our parents and caregivers so much, that we are deeply attuned to their needs, preferences, and beliefs. As adults, we find that we've unconsciously internalized many of these—including complex feelings our parents might have had about themselves and us.

As a child, both of my parents wanted me to be a high achiever, partly because they wanted me to have a good start in life and partly because of their own motivations: my father spent a lot of money on my education and wanted assurance that he had gotten his money's worth, my mother felt she would be perceived better if her daughter did well, rather than if I was merely an average student. From a young age, it was clear to me that high grades resulted in acceptance, and low grades resulted in problems. When I did well at school, music, or any other extracurricular activity, I felt accepted. When I didn't, I felt rejected, ashamed, and alone. As an adult, I struggle to take time off and not feel guilty. When it comes to self-care, part of me feels I need to earn it by working hard or achieving—just as I felt I needed to earn my parents' care (and avoid their disapproval) by working hard and achieving.

However well intentioned our parents might have been, we all grow up with beliefs about what makes us "worthy" people. By uncovering and developing an awareness of these beliefs, we're far better able to see how they affect our current lives and especially our levels of self-care.

3. Self-care feels like another obligation

We'll talk more about this in the next chapter, *Self-care and Shame*, so I'll give a quick introduction here. When we're starting or maintaining a self-care habit, we need to be careful that we're providing ourselves with regular and consistent self-care without turning that self-care into another "should." When we start feeling obligated to take time out for self-care a set number of times per week, or when we start criticizing ourselves for not having time, forgetting, or prioritizing other activities over our well-being, self-care can easily start to feel like another obligation.

Like most things we feel obligated to do, once we start telling ourselves we "should" be engaging in self-care (and all the self-judgment that comes with that "should"), our resistance to doing it will increase: guaranteed. When the balance tips and we start viewing self-care as an obligation—something we *should* be doing—the fun washes away, and we switch our energy to finding reasons why we *shouldn't* be doing it instead. When self-care feels like an obligation, we start treating it as another task on our list, instead of one of our highest priorities.

4. White knight syndrome

White knight syndrome is a state of mind Barbara Stanny talks about in her book *Overcoming Underearning*. She uses the term to describe women who are waiting for someone or something to rescue them financially. This might involve waiting to win the lottery, inherit money, or to find a partner who will take care of all their financial needs. People who experience white knight syndrome aren't always conscious of having this underlying desire or belief, but it deeply inhibits their ability to go out, carve a fulfilling and meaningful career and build a secure financial future for themselves.

Just as white knight syndrome affects women financially, this pattern plays out with self-care too. Many people, regardless of gender, struggle to express their true needs and desires. When our basic needs are either neglected or overtly rejected as children, parts of us split off and stay in a childlike state, perpetually waiting for someone else to come along and meet those unmet needs—in other words, to re-parent us.

This unconscious desire can play out for the duration of our lives if we don't process it and take responsibility for meeting our own needs. We might be aware on an intellectual level that, as adults, the time for us to be parented is long past; however, these hurt and exiled parts of us that are stuck in the past are still seeking solace and rescue. Just as we yearn for our parents and caregivers to meet our needs as children (and feel a mixture of uncomfortable and "negative" emotions when they don't), we end up yearning for someone to come along and take care of us as adults too (and feel a mixture of uncomfortable and "negative" emotions when they don't). In addition, we often want to be able to meet these needs without having to navigate the tricky social landscapes of expressing and asserting our needs, as well as negotiating how we can meet them within our relationships and interactions with others.

The truth is that *as adults, the only person who can meet your unmet needs—whether these are needs from childhood or in the present—is you.* The only person that can meet my unmet needs is me. The only person who can meet my next-door neighbor's needs is my next-door neighbor. When we become dependent on other people to guess and fulfill our needs, we are inevitably left feeling depressed, unfulfilled, and unloved. If we're not aware of this dependency, we will also feel resentful towards those we perceive as failing to meet our needs. This can have devastating effects on our relationships and deeply affects our sense of security in relation to the world around us too.

If the concept of white knight syndrome resonates with you, I admire your self-honesty. Working through this belief and taking back control over your own self-care is a challenge, but one well worth undertaking. No one will ever care about your well-being, health, and happiness as much as you do. Once we realize that, and realize that the only way to get our needs and preferences met is to take charge of meeting them ourselves, we will notice internal shifts. Most of all, we'll finally be in a place to address needs that have gone unmet for decades and begin to take action that will fulfill them.

5. Social and cultural conditioning

Social conditioning, especially gender-based social conditioning, is a huge topic, so I'm going to highlight two key social messages here that are specifically relevant to self-care. This kind of conditioning applies to both men and women. Its influence on each gender is different, but it does affect how each gender views self-care and is important to think about as you move forward with your own self-care practice.

First, *we are taught that sacrifice is virtuous.* When we put other people first, we're living up to our role as a "good little girl or boy." When we don't put other people first, we're selfish, cold hearted, and a "bad" girl or boy.

In reality, sacrifice is not virtuous. When it's done out of obligation, it breeds resentment, damages relationships, and it leaves us seething with unmet needs. Our society's praise of sacrifice ignores the fact that we're in a far better place to serve others when we've taken care of our own needs first. The notion of sacrifice is fundamentally win-lose: if Mary wants to go out to a book club one night, but Tom wants her to stay at home to meet his boss, who is coming over for drinks, the model of sacrifice would mean either Mary skipping her book club or Tom not being able to introduce his boss to his wife. In either scenario someone loses. Sacrifice overlooks the potential for *negotiation*—that both parties can get their needs met and maintain equality and harmony in the relationship.

The most sustainable way of relating to ourselves and the people around us is from a position of negotiation, not sacrifice.

Another strong cultural belief revolves around emotion, for example that *women should not get angry and men should not express sadness or hurt.* This means that many women express anger through tears and find it much easier to identify with feeling upset than angry. Equally, many men turn to anger in place of expressing pain or sadness.

How does this conditioning affect your engagement with self-care?

This conditioning leaves people cut off from certain—very human—parts of themselves. The beliefs that underlie the conditioning jar with our natural, human instincts, and can cause massive internal conflict within us. If we are feeling sad but have been conditioned to express this as anger, we won't be able to process that sadness, and it will linger and build. Equally, if we feel angry but have been conditioned to express this as sadness, we won't be able to process that anger, and it will linger and build too. Ultimately, these beliefs can lead us to resist engaging in self-care—because deep down we know that when we truly engage in self-care, *we put our needs first.* We allow ourselves to feel angry, to say no, to express our true opinions, to be real, and ultimately, to be authentic.

The prospect of being authentic and putting our needs first is both liberating and challenging. We want our freedom but, at the same time, we don't want to break the norm, step out of the mold, become the black sheep, and risk upsetting or offending those around us. We want to be loved by our families, accepted by our partners, liked by our friends, and respected by our colleagues. We fear that if we start contradicting these social norms, if we start expressing ourselves and treating ourselves as *humans* instead of culturally conditioned gender bots, we'll ultimately be rejected.

Well, we might.

Considering this possibility, the question I pose to you is: *what's right?*

Do you curb your beautiful authenticity, uniqueness, and sense of self to fit in with the herd, or do you risk displeasing a few people (who, if they're unwilling to accept you as you are, are not worth your time and energy anyway) and live a gloriously rich, fulfilling, and heartfelt life?

You can probably tell which side of the line I've fallen on. It's not an easy choice to make, but the rewards are worth it.

How to overcome resistance

1. Understand

I've spent the majority of this chapter explaining the different types of resistance and am devoting just a short section at the end to how to overcome it for a very good reason. Understanding is the first, and arguably most important, step in the process of shifting resistance.

Do what you can to learn more about your resistance: journal, talk to the resistance, ask it why it's there and what it's trying to protect you from. Notice when and how it comes up, look for patterns, and look for the logic hidden in those patterns. Our emotions are all entirely rational reactions to events and circumstances; they might be reactions to events and situations that happened in the past, but they are still rational. So give your resistance the benefit of the doubt and look for the reasons underneath.

2. Be patient

However frustrating, uncomfortable, and downright inconvenient it feels, your resistance is there for a reason. Listen, acknowledge, try to accept, and you *can* ride it out. Resistance is a process, not a state of being. Keep engaging with it, keep talking to it, and you will experience shifts.

3. Get support

You're ultimately responsible for your own self-care, but that doesn't mean you can't get support along the way. Finding a support system is especially important if you have a core belief that it's better to be independent and do everything yourself than ask for support, or if you don't have much support within your immediate circle of friends and family.

Apart from the fact that we're social creatures, and our needs for acceptance and community are two of the most fundamental human needs we have, support is just plain helpful. As you build your self-care practice, you'll be challenging long-held beliefs, changing relationship dynamics, and shifting the way you understand and interact with the world. While these changes are ultimately good, they can lead to periods of discomfort. During those moments, it makes all the difference to have a support network you can call on to provide an ear to listen, a shoulder to cry on, or someone to reflect back what they hear and see from you.

Having a supportive network is also useful when tackling resistance itself. Resistance is essentially a stuck thought pattern: While we're inside the pattern, we're going to find it hard to see beyond the pattern. Think about what happens when a car's wheels get stuck in a muddy rut. The more you try to rev the car to get out of the rut, the deeper the wheels become entrenched in the mud, and the harder it becomes to move the car. Our resistance is similar: the more we try to fight it, the deeper it becomes.

Talking to other people can be helpful as they have a more objective view of our resistance, as well as the beliefs or patterns that are playing into that resistance. While we're revving away behind the wheel of the car, they're the ones watching from a distance, observing the situation and its solutions from a perspective we don't have ourselves.

4. Accept it

In a world where "if you hate something, change something" is the prevailing motto, accepting something about ourselves that we don't like might seem counterintuitive.

But it's true.

One of the most important steps towards a shift or change lies in *accepting* the thing that you want to shift or change. We've already talked about how self-flagellation is counterproductive when it comes to creating new habits. It's also highly damaging to our relationships with ourselves.

For most of us, there's no way that we'd say the kinds of things to a friend that our inner critic says to us.

Let's imagine you're going through a stressful period in your life. You arrange to meet a friend, but you get caught up in something at work, the arrangement slips your mind, and you end up arriving one hour late. Your friend is not happy. Here are possible responses; think about how you would feel if you were at the receiving end of each as you read them:

"I can't believe you're a *whole hour* late! It's so disrespectful, you obviously don't care about this friendship otherwise you would remember when we arrange to meet up. I'd rather be friends with someone who actually gives a s*** about arrangements we make. This is the third time out of five that you've either changed the date or been late, I'm sick of being messed around by you."

Or

"I'm feeling frustrated that you were late. I do understand you have a lot going on now and you're really busy—I do believe you want us to stay in touch as friends. When you're late or change the date of our meeting several times, I feel annoyed, hurt and I notice myself wondering how important our friendship is to you. I really want us to come to some kind of arrangement that works for both of us: would you be willing to talk about this?"

Both examples might be hard to hear, but the second is far more likely to lead to a productive conversation than the first. The speaker in the second example still manages to express her feelings, but she also expresses empathy, understanding and an acceptance of where you are. The underlying message from the speaker in the first example is clear: change, or you're in trouble.

When we criticize ourselves, we harm our relationship with ourselves. Your resistance is coming from a part of you, therefore it will respond just as a person would.

All parts of us are working to protect and help us in some way, even if this isn't immediately obvious. If we're mean to our self-care resistance, reject or berate it, it will stand its ground and come back stronger than ever. If we accept it and demonstrate curiosity, understanding, and *trust* that it's trying to protect us from something (change, disharmony at home, breaking conditioned beliefs, and false childhood "truths"), we're far more likely to be able to negotiate with it.

Resistance in brief

- Resistance to self-care can be caused by the language we use around self-care, our attitude towards it, our conditioned beliefs, white knight syndrome, and our social conditioning.
- A large part of overcoming resistance rests in understanding that we alone are responsible for meeting our own needs.
- We can begin to overcome resistance by understanding its roots, showing ourselves patience, getting support, and accepting the fact that we feel resistance in the first place.

—

7

SELF-CARE AND SHAME

The decision to create your life must be based in self-kindness and fed by self-nurturing.

—Jennifer Loudon

We've talked about creating sustainable habits. We've talked about understanding and overcoming resistance. Now, we're going to talk about an idea that ties in with both of the previous chapters: shame. The ideas in this section will not only help you build a sustainable practice out of self-care, but also help you overcome resistance, without resorting to criticizing or shaming yourself.

In the introduction, I mentioned that I'm reluctant to use words like "need to," "should," and "must" when it comes to self-care. When we're "should"-ing ourselves, it's in our best interests to examine where that should is coming from and whether its genesis is a place of self-care. Some shoulds do come from a positive internal place, however we usually find that they are a result of other people's opinions and ideas and not authentically ours.

So what's wrong with these words?

Although the words "should," "need to," and "must" are well-meaning in this context, we usually use them to convey moral and social obligation. That in itself isn't the issue: *it's the consequences of not meeting those obligations* that weigh heavily on our hearts, and on our conscience, when we hear them. At some point, most of us were indoctrinated to believe that when someone tells us we "should," "need to," or "must" do something; we had better do it or face bitter consequences. This starts in childhood and continues until we internalize those beliefs ourselves. When that happens, we don't need someone to tell us how unpleasant the consequences will be if we fail to carry out any action that comes after a "should," "need to," or "must"—we have our own critical voice warning us that things will be very bad indeed if we don't.

We use these words a lot in day-to-day conversation and somewhat inaccurately. Whether many of the things we hear we "should," "need to," or "must" do are *actually* things we should, need to, or must do isn't particularly relevant here. What is relevant, and very important, is the extent to which they influence our perception of self-care. When we begin to explore the concept of self-care and start to implement it as a practice in our day-to-day lives, we tread a fine and challenging line between viewing self-care as a nurturing activity and viewing it as something else that we "should" be doing but are failing to do as often as we "should." When this happens, self-care has the potential to become a burden, another way we fail to live up to our own expectations of ourselves, and a source of internal conflict.

When we walk on the darker side of that line, self-care can start to feel like another "should" and becomes something we add to the arsenal against ourselves. And we can't take care of ourselves when we're fighting with ourselves.

Think of it this way: if we keep hanging out with someone who tells us how we should or need to be living our lives, we soon stop wanting to hang out with that person. Their "should"ing and "must"ing becomes tiring after a while, and we start to understand that their advice says more about them than it does about us.

Our internal dialogue is the same. The whole point of self-care is not to change our behavior, but to accept it. It's a bittersweet irony that change only comes about when you accept the current circumstances (remember: accepting is not necessarily equal to *liking*—we can accept things in our life without having to like them).

There is no "should" when it comes to self-care; instead, it's about desire.

It's about feeling like we are making a free *choice*. When the "shoulds" and "have-tos" creep in, that's a sign that we're acting based on unconscious beliefs and expectations rather than acting out of self-care.

When we begrudgingly force ourselves to go to that dinner, but secretly we'd rather stay home and read a book, that's a sign that we're acting based on expectation or obligation, rather than self-care. When we drag ourselves to a 90-minute yoga class because we feel we "should," we're not necessarily practicing self-care. Yes, exercise is an intrinsic part of caring for our bodies and our minds; however, it's the purpose and motivation behind the action that counts.

When we're doing things to assuage our inner critic, because we're worried about what other people will think of us, because we think we need to outperform ourselves constantly, or any other assumption that involves needing to do something to feel worthy again, we are not practicing self-care.

Right now, you might be wondering "But what if I feel resistance? Surely in those times I need to give myself a little push into doing self-care; otherwise, I'll end up letting my resistance rule."

Yes, you will feel resistance. In the moment, it might be hard to work out how to keep your self-care in balance without letting the resistance take over.

The key lies in having self-discipline without self-flagellation; in other words, in the *intention*. If you're overcoming resistance by berating yourself into a self-care practice, you're unlikely to develop a sustainable long-term self-care practice. Equally, if you're feeling resistance and letting it take control, you're also unlikely to develop a sustainable long-term self-care habit. If you can meet yourself where you're at, work to understand and accept your resistance, and focus on a positive *intention* for your self-care as the motivation for doing it, then you don't need to "should" yourself into or out of doing anything.

The danger of the "should" spiral

I struggle with using "should"s, "need-to"s, and "must"s to motivate myself, and for a long time I thought I needed to use them. I thought these words motivated me to get on with what I felt I should, needed to, or must do, and I couldn't trust myself to get anything done without using them.

The problem with motivating ourselves this way, though, is that it isn't a motivation grounded in self-worth and respect. When we "should" ourselves, not only do we communicate the inherent message that we need to change (and that we're not good enough or even acceptable as we are right now), but we also utilize a dangerous emotion that lies under the "should":

Shame.

When we view self-care as a "must" or "should" and feel ashamed when we don't act on our intentions, we create a massive block to self-care. At the root of shame is a fear that we are unlovable, unworthy, and unacceptable, which are all existentially terrifying thoughts that many us will do anything to avoid confronting. Perceiving ourselves as lovable, worthy, and acceptable is so fundamental to our happiness and mental health that feelings of shame are highly threatening to our existence and damaging to our self-esteem.

As shame and vulnerability researcher Brené Brown points out, there is a huge difference between feeling guilt and feeling shame:

"Guilt = I did something bad. Shame = I am bad."

Guilt attaches a value judgment to our behaviors or actions, while shame attaches a value judgment to *ourselves*. Feeling guilty about something is a helpful motivator for changing our behavior in the future. Feeling ashamed, however, implies that we are fundamentally flawed—and if that's the case where can we go from there? How could we possibly change?

As Dr. Brown reveals in her excellent books, *The Gifts of Imperfection* (Hazelden, 2010) and *Daring Greatly* (Gotham, 2012), shame is an unfortunate part of our culture. Many of us are taught important life lessons through the use of shame and at some point that shame becomes internalized. The more we are exposed to shame, and the more we consequently use shame on ourselves, the less worthy we feel as people, and the less likely we are to feel able to change that. Therefore, the shame cycle is highly toxic and self-perpetuating.

So how do we know if shame is affecting or influencing our self-care practice? In my experience shame shows up in two places when it comes to self-care: feeling ashamed with ourselves for resisting, procrastinating, or failing to create a habit that is good for us, and ashamed that we're the kind of person that might even need self-care in the first place. Perhaps we think that we should be able to get by just fine and manage without it, or perhaps we feel ashamed that we consciously need to make time for self-care (with the underlying belief that it should come naturally to us). Either way, all sources of self-care-related shame are important and necessary to work through before we can create a self-care practice that is going to be helpful to us.

Any shame associated with self-care is a block to self-care. Not only does it mean we're more likely to avoid doing anything self-care related (to avoid provoking feelings of shame), but if we're experiencing shame in relation to our self-care, that defeats the object of practicing self-care in the first place.

Shame is a pernicious feeling, and some of us are more susceptible to it than others. Exploring shame we experience in the context of our self-care practices can act as a gateway to exploring shame in other areas of our life too.

Indicators that we might feel shame around self-care include:

Reluctance to talk to anyone about it: Either we keep our desire for self-care a secret, or we hide our struggles and resistance from others for fear it will reflect poorly upon us.

Deep-rooted, powerful beliefs around self-care: These include the beliefs that engaging in self-care is a weak, even pathetic, thing to do, that self-care is only for spoilt, pampered people and that people who engage in self-care have too much time and money on their hands.

Deep-rooted, powerful beliefs about ourselves in relation to self-care: These include the beliefs that we haven't done enough to deserve spending time on self-care, that we're too poor for self-care, or that self-care is for older/prettier/nicer/smarter/more successful people (i.e., other people—not us).

Strong language around self-care: As you can see from the examples above, labels and judgments are rife in shame-filled beliefs. When we use this kind of language, either about ourselves, about self-care, or about other people who engage in self-care, it's a sign that at least part of us feels shame around some aspect of self-care.

Overcoming shame around self-care

The most effective way to overcome shame around self-care is to stop using shame as a teacher in *all* areas of our life. If we're susceptible to shame-based language and let it slip into one area of our life, it will spread to other areas in time.

Examine the beliefs. Shame arises out of beliefs about ourselves and the world around us. When we get to the root of the beliefs behind our shame, we can start to question them using our logic and reason. Once we start questioning them, we might realize that we don't actually agree with them and, from there, we can deconstruct them.

An important part of examining beliefs is taking time to do some archaeology and work out where certain beliefs come from. When we start to question why we have certain beliefs about the world (especially when they've been unconscious), we often find that our beliefs are internalized messages from childhood figures like parents, teachers, friends, and other important people. Once we recognize that, we're better able to separate out internalized beliefs that actually belong to other people from our own true beliefs and values.

Change the language. Notice when you're using judgmental and shaming language about other people, or when you have particularly strong feelings about other people's behavior when it doesn't really affect you. Also notice the difference between your own feelings of guilt and shame. Make it a conscious process to turn the latter into the former: instead of labeling yourself or someone else ("I am bad," "They are bad"), focus on the actions ("I did a bad thing," "They did a bad thing").

Empathize, empathize, empathize. Once we start changing our language and shifting from judgment and shaming to a more objective, self-aware and compassionate view of ourselves and others, we're in a better position to empathize with our own feelings of shame, either in the past or the present. Empathy is the antidote to shame: when we show ourselves empathy or open ourselves up to empathy from other people, we are saying "I am understandable; I am relatable, I am acceptable." When we begin to internalize these three beliefs, shame cannot survive.

PART 2

Starting With the Present

8

THINGS AS THEY ARE PART 1: OBSERVATIONS

With any lifestyle change, we need to be able to take a good, honest look at where we are right now so we know what kind of foundation we're working with and how best to move forward from here.

Where are we in regards to our self-care?

Before we start, I want to clarify that there is no judgment attached to the answer to this question. It's just an observation. There is no place you "should" be in your self-care, nor any right or wrong answers. Please remember that as you read through this chapter. The less judging we are of ourselves, the more we are able to accept reality as it stands and build a sustainable and fulfilling practice from there.

Below, you'll find three sets of questions. These are split into three groups according to how much time you might need to spend answering each group and how challenging you might find them. These questions are not easy. If you can work your way through these questions, answering them honestly and as fully as possible, you will truly have earned your black belt self-care ninja status.

Dedicate time to answer these questions. The knowledge you'll gain from taking time to consider them will directly affect where your self-care goes from here. Give yourself space to sit, ponder, ruminate on them, and answer as fully as you can. The answers might not always be comfortable, but we need to know where we currently are before we can work out where we want to be.

"White belt" starter questions

Let's begin with a few questions inspired by Jennifer Louden, author of *Comfort Secrets for Busy Women* (Sourcebooks, 2003). These questions are designed to help you look at where your self-care is right now, the things that are stopping you from engaging in self-care as fully as you might like, and to start to explore what you might do to change things around to get your needs met. When answering these questions, think about your life over the course of an average week—from the first thing on Monday morning, to the last thing on Sunday night.

1. *What situations, commitments, relationships, obligations, or things prevent me from relaxing and engaging in self-care?*

2. *Which of these things am I choosing to engage in?*

3. *What can I do to reduce the influence and impact of these things on my self-care?*

Once you've answered the above questions as fully as possible, move on to the questions below. These questions are designed to help you move forward. Gaining awareness about the things that might stop us from engaging in self-care is the first part of the process. Learning how to recognize the feelings, patterns, and behaviors that appear when we haven't been engaging in self-care helps us to become better able to regulate our self-care practice in a way that works for us and meets our needs.

4. *What are the symptoms that I haven't been engaging in self-care?*

5. *Which of those signs have I seen in the past week or two?*

6. *How can I use the information within these signs to right my internal balance and focus more on my self-care?*

7. *What fears do I have about self-care?*

"Blue belt" intermediate questions

These questions might be slightly more challenging to answer than the previous set, and they require more thought and time. *But they are still necessary.* Set aside 15 to 20 minutes where you can sit down and focus on answering these questions as fully as possible. Laying this groundwork now will provide you with a stronger foundation from which to look at your self-care practices.

To start, we're going to think of two particular sensations: anxiety and discomfort. These are human emotions to feel, yet often we try to avoid feeling them (or even acknowledging that we feel them).

8. *All of our emotions send us a message, trying to tell us something about where we are at that moment. Think about when you feel stress: what is it telling you?*

9. *Discomfort is a sign of desired change. What is your discomfort telling you?*

The next questions are about time and the choices we make with our time. Our time is so precious to us, yet often we don't understand just how much control or power we have over how we spend our time and what we do with it. This isn't because we're not grateful for the time we have, but because we aren't always conscious of how we're using it (and whether we're using it in a way that is best for us).

10. *How do I organize my time right now?*

11. *What are the principles behind how I organize my time?*

12. *Do I organize my time from a feeling of obligation or choice?*

Now we're going to shift the focus of these questions to giving and receiving care. Most of us can identify with being very good at giving care, but we might struggle to be open and willing when receiving it. Somewhat ironically, the reality is that we cannot truly give others the care that we cannot, or are unwilling to, receive ourselves. Even if we feel more comfortable giving it than receiving it, if we feel uncomfortable receiving it then we're not going to be the best caregivers we can be in the first place! Therefore, becoming more aware of where we are in regard to receiving care, and how it feels to receive care, will improve our relationships with others, and how cared for they feel by us, too.

13. *How good am I at receiving care, either from myself or others?*

14. *When I think about times when I have been cared for, how does that feel?* (This could be a mixture of comfortable and uncomfortable feelings)

"Black belt" advanced questions

Now we're into the black-belt ninja level of self-care. The following questions are hard. I say that to encourage you, rather than to discourage you. Give them a go, and you're already engaging in one of the most challenging aspects of self-care: facing up to truth and reality as it stands. You might not be able to answer these questions immediately. After all, they're designed to draw out unconscious knowledge into our conscious space. Instead, consider each of them in turn, let each question percolate for as long as it needs, and start formulating an answer with notes, words, or phrases. You don't need a fully formed answer at this stage; instead, just start writing down your ideas in response to each question when they come.

15. *What realities am I ignoring?*

16. *What thing in my life provokes fear, dread, worry, anxiety, or a longing for change, but I keep ignoring it or telling myself it will be OK?* (This could be money, a relationship, your job, your sense of purpose in life, or obligations you don't want).

17. *What message am I sending to the universe? Do I constantly feel like, and portray myself as, a victim? Do I dwell on negatives at the expense of positives? Am I generally optimistic?*

18. *What does my body language say about where I'm at? Do I communicate my feelings of self-doubt through my speech and body language, or do I engage with the world with self-belief and brightness?*

19. *What do my decisions say about where I am? What do my behaviors and life choices say to other people about my feelings of self-worth, my sense of self-value and how I perceive my place in the world?*

Remember that none of the answers to these questions are right, wrong, good, or bad. Whatever the answers are, that's where you are. Like I said at the beginning of the chapter, the purpose of these questions isn't to encourage you to judge yourself, or feel ashamed of where you're at right now. It's an observation, not an evaluation.

The questions above are challenging. They force our brains to work in different ways than we might be used to, and they can bring up uncomfortable feelings and realizations too. If you start feeling uncomfortable, do not skip this section. Take breaks if you need to, but make sure you give every question in this chapter the attention that it needs. You'll be thankful later; I promise.

We're going to end with one final question. Again, you don't have to answer this now; it's designed more to plant a seed in your mind—one that will germinate and grow as you move through this book.

20. *What does your "best self" look like to you?*

9

THINGS AS THEY ARE PART 2: THE GROUNDWORK

Now that we're through the tough questions, it's time to take a step back and look at what you're already doing that works for you—and what you're doing that doesn't. Just like the last chapter, taking enough time to work through the following in as much detail as possible will provide you with a helpful foundation on which you can build a nurturing and fulfilling self-care practice.

Once again, the aim of the following content is to notice, not to judge.

Mapping your current self-care routine

Now that we've looked at the difference between self-care practices and coping strategies, here is your first question:

What self-care practices do you already do?

When you want to reconnect with yourself, make sure you're meeting unmet needs and nurture yourself in both the present and the future, what do you do? It could be as simple as switching off the computer and reading a good book, enjoying a lie-in, or making time to prepare a home cooked meal. It could also be bigger: attending a meditation retreat, booking a stay at a spa (although not if it hurts you financially—remember that all your needs are important), or taking time away from situations that aren't serving you.

Much of the time, we do these things without even being aware that we're engaging in self-care. Taking the time to identify what you're already doing that works gives you a starting point from which you can build a deeper and stronger self-care practice. (Remember that coping strategies aren't true self-care practices so don't belong on this list.)

To give you a helping hand, here's a prompt from Jennifer Loudon's excellent book *The Life Organizer: A Woman's Guide to A Mindful Year* (New World Library, 2007) to get you started:

"'Without ____ I would be lost.' Spend as long as you need filling in all the blanks. Then, choose the top three. Without these things you would be lost. These are the things you really need to stay sane, stay connected to yourself, and to not completely lose yourself in the outside world."

When I did this exercise, I discovered that my three sanity must-haves were:

Time alone

A journal and pen

Enough sleep

What would fill your blanks?

Mapping your current coping routine

What coping strategies do you currently use?

What behaviors do you currently engage in that are designed to meet one or more of your needs but do so at the expense of one or more of your other needs? Acknowledging our coping strategies can be challenging, so know that you are incredibly brave to do so.

Building this awareness doesn't mean judging it or criticizing ourselves. If we do those things, we are far less likely to acknowledge reality as it is, and far more likely to shy away from the truth. If, however, we can approach our experience with an open mind, compassion, and acceptance of reality—even if it feels painful—we are far more likely to open ourselves up to the truth. We're also in a better position to align our current selves with our best selves.

Here's a prompt that might help you when thinking about your coping strategies:

When I am being totally honest with myself, I acknowledge that I feel compelled to do _____ when I feel _____.

Fill this out as many times as you need to pay due care and attention to your coping strategies.

10

GETTING TO THE NEEDS

Now that you've done the hard work and evaluated where you are with your self-care in the present, let's start to identify some of the needs we can meet using genuine self-care practices.

As I explained earlier, we can only be the best version of ourselves—inside and out—when we are in touch with, and meeting, our needs. Coping mechanisms get in the way of this, as they provide an immediate relief from the discomfort or pain caused by the unmet need (like slapping a Band-Aid on it), but they don't meet the need in the long term. The most effective way to switch from coping to caring is to replace one with the other.

Many of the needs underlying these coping strategies are similar, but the exact needs behind your coping strategies will be personal and could be completely different compared to the needs of the next person reading this book. Although I've listed the needs that resonate with me (and that I can imagining resonating for others) within the context of each coping strategy, this list is not at all definitive. It's essential that you take the time to work out *what your core needs are and how you can best meet them* for yourself.

This task is more than a one-time activity, as it involves deepening our self-awareness. Self-awareness is a lifetime process: there are no shortcuts. If we try to take shortcuts, we end up missing out on valuable self-knowledge. Discovering your core needs is a huge topic that goes beyond the scope of this book. I've created a living list of helpful resources to accompany this book on my website, Becoming Who You Are (*www.becomingwhoyouare.net/fctt-resources*), and I encourage you to seek support from a counsellor, coach, or other helping professional who can assist you in identifying obscured or buried needs and desires.

Just as our preferences change over time, our needs change over time too. Things that weren't so important to us become more important as we grow older and gain more life experience. Equally, other things that once felt important might not feel so important in time. Therefore, it's important for us to maintain a dialogue with ourselves, to check in with our experiences, and to keep searching inside for what it is we need at any given time.

You can only gain this kind of knowledge through self-dialogue and self-awareness. It's not the kind of information you can gain from a book, but the good news is that the information you need is there, waiting for you to hear it.

To get started, I've taken the questions from the first chapter and listed some of the needs I think might be behind these behaviors. As a guide, I've referred to the Needs Inventory available on the Center for Nonviolent Communication website (we'll be talking more about the concept of Nonviolent Communication and how it can be helpful to us later in the book).

This list is not exhaustive. You might be able to identify other needs that some of these behaviors Band-Aid for you. As you read the rest of this section, think about which needs resonate with you and which you would add yourself. For each question, I list the broad needs we might be trying to meet with these behaviors and a description of how the behavior might meet these needs underneath.

How can I...

Stop watching so much TV?

Needs: Acceptance (including self-acceptance), relaxation, intellectual stimulation, companionship, self-expression

Spending an excessive amount of time watching TV is a great distraction from real life. I got rid of my TV four years ago, partly because I realized what an inordinate amount of time I spent zoning out in front of it. Don't get me wrong: I still appreciate TV and movies. I keep track of programs I like, and I catch up with these online or on DVD. The difference is that I'm not watching for the sake of watching; I don't channel surf, and I don't use it as a way to dissociate from any uncomfortable feelings or issues at the end of a rough day.

So what needs does "so much TV" meet? It's a great way to distract ourselves. It provides us with peace away from conflicting or critical internal dialogue. It also draws us away from side projects that might be far more meaningful to us, but that our inner dialogue tells us are too big/difficult/outside our comfort zone right now (a need for *self-acceptance*).

We might want to relax in a safe haven away from the stresses and strains of other areas of our life (*relaxation*). We might want to learn and grow, and we try to get our need for *intellectual stimulation* met through television documentaries and news programs. We might be lonely, and the sounds and images on TV help us feel less alone (a need for *companionship*).

Perhaps we're wary of how we would feel if we weren't distracted by TV. We sense that many challenging thoughts and feelings might occur that could be very uncomfortable indeed, so we drown them out by getting lost in other people's stories. The emotions are still there waiting to come out, but we are scared by how uncomfortable they might feel, so we avoid them (a need for *self-expression*).

Cut down my drinking?

Needs: Acceptance (including self-acceptance), physical health, relaxation, self-expression, belonging, sexual expression, rest and sleep, ease, spontaneity, peace, companionship, creativity, inspiration

Alcohol is an effective coping mechanism for most of the above needs for one main reason: it has a chemical effect that lowers our inhibitions, leaves us feeling able to speak and act more freely, leaves us feeling more relaxed, calms our internal chatter and self-criticism, and helps us go to sleep (though our quality of sleep is usually poorer after drinking).

Drinking is a very social activity. Meetings with friends or family might revolve around going to a pub or bar and whiling away an evening over a few beers or more. Drinking is such a mainstay, especially in British culture, that not participating can lead to awkward questions and peer pressure.

Then there's the pervasive cultural myth that drinking helps get our creative juices flowing. As a writer, I've met many people who have come to rely on alcohol to 'get creative,' no doubt fueled by romanticized ideas of successful creatives like Hemingway. Perhaps they can write, paint, compose, or create more freely, but there are other ways to meet their need for *creativity, inspiration*, and *self-expression*.

Stop spending so much money?

Needs: Appreciation, autonomy, love, intimacy, belonging, affection, beauty, spontaneity, hope, stimulation, participation, to matter

On a broad level, spending money falls into two categories: spending money on ourselves and spending money on other people. Spending money in itself isn't a bad thing (after all, what else is it there for?). The problems arise when we spend money on ourselves and other people in a way that conflicts with our need for security or stability and in a way that harms our future selves financially.

We might overspend on others out of a need for *appreciation, participation, to matter,* and *belonging.* Perhaps we use financial gifts or largesse as an attempt to secure someone's friendship or retain favor with family members. Alternatively, we might overspend on ourselves as a way to demonstrate our *autonomy* when we don't feel in control of other areas of our life, to feel *affection*—even if we're the ones buying ourselves gifts, and to keep up with the Joneses—another type of *participation* and *belonging.* Money can also buy a range of products that we might use to meet our need for *beauty, hope,* or *stimulation.*

Stop smoking?

Needs: Physical health, relaxation, stimulation, belonging, (self-)acceptance, support, inclusion

Like drinking, smoking is one of those habits that are ingrained within our lifestyle. We might use it as a method of *relaxation* when we're feeling stressed, anxious, or when we're struggling to meet need for *(self-)acceptance.* We might also use it as a pick-me-up when we're feeling bored or tired. If we're surrounded by friends and family who also smoke, it's harder to quit as we might have a need for *inclusion* and *belonging.* Ultimately, using smoking as a coping mechanism could signify a need for *support.* It's important to identify the underlying needs and find healthier substitutes, especially if you're aware of your need for *physical health.*

Get fitter?

Needs: Physical health, energy, sleep, movement, challenge, awareness, growth, nurturing, self-respect, ease

This question is tricky, as there are two types of needs that come into play here. We all know that exercise is good for us on a logical level, and we might have the desire to start a healthy exercise habit, but starting and sticking to a consistent exercise regime is far from easy. All the needs listed above apply to why we might *want* to become more fit, but what about the needs that mean we struggle to do this?

Speaking from experience, my biggest resistance to regular exercise comes from my need for *comfort.* We're going to talk about exercise in the next section so I won't go into too much detail here. All you need to do right now is to think about what is stopping you from fulfilling your desire to become more fit: what does your internal dialogue say about it? And what are the needs underneath that dialogue?

Eat more healthily?

Needs: Comfort, control, acceptance (and self-acceptance), love, beauty, physical well-being, affection, closeness, companionship, intimacy, consciousness, understanding

The way we approach our eating habits is another topic I'm going to include in the next chapter, so, like exercise, I'll just touch on it briefly here.

When we have a desire to eat more healthily, this might be because we feel we are eating too much, we are eating foods that don't serve our health in the long run, or because we are eating too little. We might desire to change the kinds of foods we eat out of a need for *physical well-being, consciousness,* and *understanding.*

At the same time, we might currently limit what we eat in an attempt to meet unmet needs like *control, love, beauty, acceptance,* and *self-acceptance.* Equally, if our eating habits are causing poor health, we might desire to eat less out of a need for all the above.

These desires can also stem from needs like *comfort, closeness,* and *companionship.* When we use food as a way to meet needs that are separate from our physical well-being, it can be harder to change our eating habits. We might eat too much, or turn to foods that induce a chemical high (namely sugar and carbs) to quell uncomfortable feelings like anxiety, loneliness, or a lack of acceptance (*self-acceptance or external acceptance*). When this happens, it's much harder to eat in a way that is truly beneficial to us and much harder to change our eating habits to ones that might serve our health in the long term too.

Experience a richer social life?

Needs: Connection, community, empathy, to understand and be understood, to see and to be seen, acceptance, belonging, inclusion, support, to know and to be known, trust, stability, warmth, presence, play, joy, contribution, growth, participation, understanding, stimulation, to matter

Although the above needs might leave us desiring a richer social life than we currently have, many of the same needs might be holding us back from pursuing this.

Perhaps we fear judgment from our current social circle, perhaps we fear stepping outside of our comfort zone in an effort to meet new people, or being rejected. Maybe we don't find our current social life particularly stimulating or fulfilling, and part of us fears that, after going through the vulnerability and risk of broadening that circle, we might not find the stimulation or fulfillment we want anyway. This leaves us paralyzed, trapped in a situation that isn't serving our needs, yet feeling unable to do anything to change it.

Get enough sleep?

Needs: Sleep/rest, energy, awareness, efficacy, ease

Like exercising and eating well, we know sleep is essential for our sense of well-being and our ability to be the best version of ourselves. Yet we might still struggle to fill our sleep quota, maybe because our desire for *efficacy* takes priority, and we sacrifice our sleep for other activities. We might also find our need for *security* or *stability* interfering with our need for sleep. Perhaps there are things that are happening in our lives right now that provoke anxiety and start running through our minds as soon as our heads hit the pillow.

We might also struggle to get enough sleep because we are struggling to meet the needs I talked about in response to "How can I stop watching so much TV?" When we try to distract ourselves from some needs (for example, a need for *self-expression*), we unwittingly distract ourselves from other needs in the process, too—in this case, the needs listed above. We stay up late in front of the TV, computer screen, or just generally pottering around, to distract ourselves from whatever we don't want to address. Before we know it, it's one or two a.m.

This can also happen if we're trying to avoid feeling discomfort about something happening the next day. If we're dreading going into work, dreading something we need to do, or dreading something that's going to happen, we might stay up late and avoid sleep as a way of 'delaying' the inevitable occurrence (of course, anything we feel anxiety about is much more easily faced when we are well-rested and fully conscious). In this way, a desire for more sleep, matched with the recognition that we're not getting enough sleep, can indicate disharmony in other areas of our lives too.

Reduce my busyness?

Needs: Relaxation, closeness, nurturing, self-respect, support, rest, play, choice, freedom, creativity, contribution, effectiveness, efficacy, learning, purpose, participation, stimulation, to matter

Busyness is a chronic condition of our world today. Many of us would love to be less busy, yet at the same time we're not making the decisions we need to make to achieve that.

We often feel like we *have* to do certain things, when really we're *choosing* to do them—we're just not taking responsibility for that decision. We yearn for more time to relax, connect to ourselves, and look after ourselves (*relaxation, closeness, nurturing, self-respect, support, rest*).

We might also be able to identify other things we want to do with our time, instead of feeling obligated to fill it with tasks and activities that don't meet our needs (*play, choice, freedom*).

We might use our busyness to meet needs like *creativity, contribution, effectiveness, efficacy, learning, purpose, participation, stimulation*, and *to matter*. But when we use busyness to meet these needs, we do so at the expense of other important needs—one of the self-care no-nos.

The key to reclaiming our time is to find another way to meet these needs or reframe our perspective on what fulfilling these needs would look like in the first place.

Improve my relationships?

Needs: Acceptance, affection, closeness, belonging, empathy, intimacy, love, mutuality, respect, stability, support, to know and be known, to see and be seen, to understand and be understood, trust, warmth, authenticity, integrity, harmony, joy, freedom, growth, hope, self-expression, to matter, understanding

Engaging in relationships that aren't serving our needs might sound like a counterintuitive coping strategy, but it most certainly is one. When we're involved in relationships that don't fulfill us, we have something to focus on and something to fix. When we're focused on an external entity, such as another person or the partnership overall, we are distracted from focusing on our own internal challenges, conflicts and growth. In other words, staying in, and dealing with, relationships that don't serve our needs can be a great way to avoid personal growth.

Many people argue the opposite of this. They would say that our strength comes from resolving challenging relationships and learning to live with people we find difficult. I strongly disagree. The people closest to us have a huge influence on our internal dialogue, and you want to make sure that internal dialogue is healthy and supportive. In addition, life is far too short and our time too precious to spend it in situations or with people that don't help us meet our needs.

Our involvement in relationships that don't serve us—whether a romantic relationship, a friendship, or family relationship—also slaps a Band-Aid over the same kinds of needs I listed under "Experience a Richer Social Life?" Perhaps there's a little voice telling us that we'd be lonely, that this is what we deserve, that we're not smart or good enough to be around people who would treat us better, or that people wouldn't accept our authentic selves—we'd never be able to be free. This is a tough voice to hear, but it's there for your protection. It stops you growing bigger, being rejected, hurt, and abandoned, and feeling hurt and lonely as a result.

I can't emphasize this enough: *who we surround ourselves with is so, so important.* If we want to be the best version of ourselves, staying in relationships that don't meet our needs is one of the most important coping strategies to overcome.

[Insert your own questions here]

Over the course of the next week or so, look at your own behavior. Are there any additional quick fix "slap a Band-Aid on it" coping strategies you recognize in your day-to-day life? If so, write them down, alongside any thoughts you have about why they've developed and the core needs underneath.

And relax...

Phew, that's a lot of groundwork to cover right there. I found answering these questions myself insightful and rewarding, but not always pleasant. Surveying our personal landscapes in this kind of way can shed light on some things we've been avoiding, bring to the surface other things that lay below our line of consciousness, and reveal all the coping strategies we've been using to get by until now.

That kind of clarity is not easy, and I admire your courage and dedication to meeting your needs.

Now that we've spent some time surveying our personal landscapes, looking at the most common coping strategies and uncovering needs behind them, it's time to move on to the next section: a selection of self-care suggestions you can use to kick these coping strategies to the curb once and for all. These practices will focus on meeting our needs, right to the core.

Ultimately, they will be the building blocks underneath the best possible version of yourself.

PART 3

Self-care Essentials

INTRODUCTION

You have to create with what you've been given, rather than obsess about what you wish you'd been given.

—Jennifer Louden

In the following sections, you'll find a wide variety of practices you can add to your self-care toolkit. We're going to start with suggestions that focus on ways we can meet our basic human needs. These are absolutely crucial to our experience of the world around us, our quality of life, and our overall levels of satisfaction and happiness. Notice that I said basic *human* needs; these are common needs that are shared by people everywhere, whatever their background, life experiences, or social status. If you think you're exempt from the self-care practices we're going to discuss in this section, think again.

The suggestions in this section cover aspects of self-care like sleep, food, exercise, and community—in other words, long-term self-care—and provide guidance around what we need to do to meet our most basic needs. These needs are the foundations of our self-care. Just like a building needs strong foundations, our self-care also requires strong foundations, and the practices in the following section will provide just that.

When life gets busy or we face challenging times, we slip into survival mode. When this happens, it's easy for us to neglect our most basic needs. We scrimp on sleep, we comfort eat, we overspend or tighten our purse strings, sometimes to self-punishing levels. We prioritize other things over our health and sanity. In the moment, it might feel like we need to do this to get through a rough patch, however, for our long-term health and happiness, it's important that we re-prioritize as quickly as possible.

Although some of the following self-care suggestions might sound obvious, boring, or mundane (and not really like "self-care" as you've previously thought about it at all), *these practices are the most important self-care practices of them all.* They affect us physically, mentally, and emotionally. When we are engaged in these practices, and they hold a high priority in our lives, we are at our physical, mental, and emotional best. When they are lacking, our physical, mental, and emotional well-being suffer.

So read the following self-care essentials carefully and ask yourself as honestly as possible:

Which of these practices could I engage in more?

Why am I not engaging in them more fully right now?

What needs to change for me to engage in them more fully?

What actionable steps can I start taking today to meet these needs?

12

SLEEP

Needs: Rest/sleep, presence, ease, awareness, clarity, consciousness, efficacy, effectiveness

Sleep is one of the most fundamental needs we have, yet it is often one of the first to be overlooked in times of stress and busyness. Even though it's one of the basic things we need to function, we often push sleep down our list of priorities, behind early starts, late nights, and full schedules.

But as we all know deep down, sleep is vital. We've all experienced feeling sleep deprived, and we all know that it's incredibly unpleasant. Most of the time, we try to get enough sleep to stave off or dim that zombie feeling, but many of us know in our hearts that we're not meeting this crucial need as fully as we could.

Most people find themselves in the grey area between well-rested and exhausted at one point or another. This grey area arises when we're not getting enough sleep to fulfill our natural sleep requirements; however, we're not getting so little sleep that we're at a stage of exhaustion either. We function reasonably well, so there's no overt cause for concern. Over time, this grey area between well-rested and exhausted becomes the norm: we forget what it feels like to get the amount of sleep our bodies need each night. In this place, we assume our tired-but-not-exhausted state is how we usually feel; however, in reality, we're missing out on our true levels of energy and vitality.

How it works

According to sleep researchers, most adults need between seven and nine hours of sleep a night. In fact, the amount of sleep we actually need is different for individuals. Your job is to conduct a two-week experiment that will enable you to work out your personal sleep quota.

To work out how much sleep you need, try waking up without an alarm for two weeks.

During these two weeks, if you need to make sure you get up by a set time, go to bed earlier. If you really, really need to make sure you get up, then set an alarm for the last possible moment, but *do not rely on it.*

At first, if you are sleep deprived, your body will compensate for a lack of sleep on previous nights (so perhaps start this experiment at a weekend when you have a chance to catch up on your sleep). By the end of the second week, though, you should have a much better idea about your natural sleep need. You will find yourself waking up like clockwork after the same amount of sleep each day, and you should be able to calculate what time you need to go to sleep each night to wake up alarm free.

Remember, it's about priorities. What is more important: a fully functioning body or a fully functioning alarm clock?

Why it works

Sleep affects us on both a physical and emotional level. When we are consistently getting enough sleep, the positive effects are numerous. Our bodies function more efficiently, our digestion improves, we recover from illnesses and injuries quicker, our metabolism picks up, and more. Emotionally, we are more likely to feel positive, we are more resilient to stress and anxiety; we can think more clearly, and we are less likely to turn to coping mechanisms to deal with uncomfortable feelings.

As useful as it is, electricity is a blight on our sleep. Thanks to the discovery of the electric current, we can now use artificial daylight to stay up later and use our alarm clocks to get us up again the next day. This makes it very easy to overlook how much sleep we need to be healthy. Going back to basics and ditching the alarm is a great way of resetting that pattern and getting back in touch with your needs and natural rhythm again.

13

EXERCISE

Those who think they have not time for bodily exercise will sooner or later have to find time for illness.

—*Edward Stanley*

Needs: Movement, self-respect, participation, belonging, play, spontaneity, challenge, contribution, growth, learning, stimulation

Just like food and money, exercise is the foundation for our overall self-care practice. Like food and money, exercise can fall into the same dread-provoking category of "habits we need to sort out." For many of us, exercise is one of those things that we think we *should* be doing regularly, but it's a challenge.

We've already talked about several reasons why we might feel resistance to developing 'healthy' habits, so if you feel resistance when it comes to exercise, you might find it helpful to return to the chapter on *Resistance* to see if any of them resonate here.

In this section, I want to touch on a new basis for resistance that can show up when it comes to exercise: *how we perceive the task at hand.*

What do you think of when you think about the term exercise?

Intense aerobics sessions, hour-long runs, struggling to get to that ~~twentieth~~ fourth push-up?

Ultimately, what all the above examples involve is *being in a place of uncomfortable exertion for much longer than you want.*

That's one of the most common demotivating factors of regular exercise: the discomfort. Of course, we know logically that the discomfort might not feel good, but it's good *for* us. When it comes to doing exercise, however, our lizard brains don't care. We can find every excuse in the book why exercising right now would not be a good plan because we (understandably) have a basic instinct to avoid feeling discomfort.

But the fact is that exercise *is* good for us and is a crucial part of our long-term self-care. So to make this self-care activity an important part of our lives, we need to find a balance between honoring the part of ourselves that doesn't enjoy the discomfort and getting our bodies moving.

How it works

Your challenge is to get creative and find something that fits the criteria in the paragraph above. This doesn't require you to attend classes (although you can if you want), create a routine (ditto), or keep pushing yourself to go faster or longer. We're not training for a half marathon here; we're just incorporating some healthy movement and physical vitality into our lives.

Therefore:

The most important thing is that it's fun.

Yes, fun. And fun exercise does exist, I promise (see *Party like it's 1999* in the next section for an example).

As you read this, you might already have a few ideas around how you can seek out exercise in a way that feels fun but still gets your blood pumping.

In *How to Create Sustainable Habits*, I talked about BJ Fogg's *Tiny Habits* program. You can apply his approach to many different self-care activities, and exercise is particularly well-suited to the anchor-action framework.

When I signed up to BJ's course, one of my tiny habits was doing three sit-ups every time I sent an email. Before you know it, 10 emails a day equals 30 sit-ups a day, 20 emails a day equals 60. But the trick is that it's not the same as going to the gym and doing 60 sit-ups in one go. Because who really wants to do that? You do three and enjoy the cumulative effects. It's a win-win situation: you get moving, without the discomfort.

I'm aware that some professionals would argue that you need to push yourself past your comfort zone to reap the true benefits of exercise. As I already mentioned, though, we're not training for anything here. The purpose of incorporating exercise into your life is to: a) bend, stretch, and get your heart rate pumping a little harder, and b) Do so in a way that is fun and therefore sustainable.

Why it works

We all know exercise is good for us. We hear about the benefits of regular exercise from our doctors, in newspapers, magazines, online, on the TV, and most other information sources available. This isn't a lecture (and I'm not a physician) so I'm not going to reiterate what you probably already know about the effects of exercise on our sleep, blood pressure, mood, and so on.

I do want to talk about two other benefits of exercise that often get overlooked. First, exercise gives us a chance to express ourselves in a different way. It helps us connect to the physical sensations we feel in our body, and it exposes us to new experiences that we might not otherwise have. Having developed the self-concept that I'm somewhat lacking in the coordination department, you wouldn't have seen me dead at a dance class—until I tried Zumba. If I hadn't been consciously looking for fun ways to exercise, I wouldn't have discovered that, far from being the humiliating experience I imagined, dancing is actually something I really enjoy. The phrase "you don't know until you try it" is a cliché, and that's because it's true.

Importantly, possibly *most* importantly, exercise does wonders for our sense of self-efficacy. After all, when we exercise, we're sending ourselves the message that our health is worth spending time on, and we reaffirm that we are dedicated to taking care of ourselves and caring for ourselves.

14

GOOD FOOD

Needs: Acceptance, affection, companionship, compassion, consistency, consideration, nurturing, self-respect, food, water, harmony, choice, freedom, awareness, celebration of life, consciousness, understanding

As you work your way through this book, you'll notice several hot topics come up in the context of self-care. These are the topics I hear about time and time again. More often than not, they're fraught with emotion. On the surface, they are purely practical matters (and, one could argue, they ought to stay that way). Deep down, however, we attach all kinds of meaning and significance to them. They are the most common Band-Aids we use to assuage uncomfortable feelings.

In this chapter, we're going to talk about one of the biggest coping mechanisms of all:

Food

Food is complicated because, like money, there is an aspect of pleasure involved, as well as practical benefit. Because we get pleasure from eating certain foods, we can easily slip into using this pleasure to compensate for a lack of pleasure elsewhere in our lives. To add to that already-complicated relationship, we hear a lot of conflicting advice about which foods are good for us and which are bad. Wherever you turn, you'll find an alternate perspective on food. High fat versus Low fat, vegan versus Meat-based, Paleo, juicing, fasting—the list goes on.

All this choice and conflict makes it a lot easier to just avoid the question of food and diet altogether, or flit between one fad and the next, putting our bodies through a punishing regime of one diet after another.

We forgo what our bodies tell us and place the latest advice as the top priority. We get into a cycle of denial and reward. We know the connection between our diet and our appearance, and we blame ourselves and blame food for the fact we don't like the way we look. The more we think like this, the more emotionally significant food becomes and the more of a turbulent, high-stakes subject it becomes too.

In some ways, food is just like air: we need it to survive and the quality we ingest will affect our quality of life. Sometimes, we're breathing good air; sometimes we're breathing bad air. We can tell the difference between breathing bad and good air (if you've ever blown your nose after using the London Underground, you'll know what I mean), but we don't get all worked up between the different kinds of air, or spend our hard-earned money on trying out the latest air mixture for optimum health and wellness.

Of course, this analogy is limited: breathing unadulterated countryside air is pleasant and all, but it's no match for something like a chocolate, amaretto, and coconut crepe. The taste and texture of food, not counting its physiological effects, can bring us an enormous amount of pleasure (as well as an enormous amount of post-crepe regret).

So we have this complex, tangled web of feelings around food. And all the while, everything we eat affects our health, our mood, our future health and, ultimately our longevity. Because what we put into our bodies *does matter*, and it's one of the most fundamental aspects of our self-care.

A small caveat: I don't want to give the impression that I'm completely sorted when it comes to food. I'm not. I also want to avoid giving diet advice, as I'm not qualified to do so. I wrote this section as what we put into our bodies is a huge part of our self-care, and I want to share some practices that I've found helpful when it comes to my own relationship with food. If you have questions about your diet and health, please speak to your doctor or trained nutritionist to get more in-depth and professionally informed answers.

How it works

1. Education

We put food into our bodies every day and the kinds of foods we eat deeply affect our quality of life. Therefore, it's important to educate yourself about which foods are best to eat and why.

Whether you enjoy learning through books, videos, online articles, or any other format, you can find a wealth of information about nutrition and which foods are good for you, either for free or at a low cost.

As a general rule, the greater the ratio of natural, whole foods to processed, manufactured foods in our diets, the better. Enjoy 'clean' eating, where fresh trumps canned or dried, go easy on the carbohydrates, and enjoy the protein. Avoid addictive substances (like sugar and caffeine—more on that below) and use a rule that's my personal favorite: if you can't pronounce one of more ingredients, it's probably not a good idea to eat it.

2. Cut the addictions

As I mentioned at the beginning of this section, food does bring us pleasure; however there are different *kinds* of pleasure at play. For example, there is a difference between the kind of pleasure involved in eating the above chocolate, amaretto, and coconut crepe and eating a wholesome bowl of papaya with coconut and natural yoghurt (my favorite Mexican breakfast). When faced with a showdown between the two, no matter how much I love papaya (and I do, so much), I'm still going to be tempted by the crepe, because sugar is completely and utterly addictive.

The latest evidence for why we're such sugar junkies suggests that the answer lies in a combination of evolutionary factors (sugar is a great source of fast-burning energy but, before industrialized agriculture, a scarcity) and the delightful chemical effects that sugar has on our bodies. These effects are so heady that when the next cake opportunity comes around, we're far more likely to remember and crave the taste and sugar high, than we are to remember and heed the regretful waddle home and sugar crash that came after the last overindulgence.

This doesn't just apply to sugar; it applies to things like caffeine, alcohol, and carbs in general (which are, themselves, a form of sugar). The vast majority of us have the potential to be addicted to one or more of these things on one level or another (myself included). And addictions are a barrier to both our authentic selves and genuine self-care.

So how do you develop an awareness of these addictions and regain control over your body? It's a continual process, but the three steps below will help.

3. Listen to your body

Your body tells you everything you need to know about the quality of your diet and how conducive it is to your self-care. As I mentioned above, eating cake, chocolate, ice cream, a giant cookie, or whatever your sugar-fest of choice might be, feels awesome in the moment. Afterwards, however, comes the inevitable sugar crash. We feel cranky; we want to sleep and usually we respond to this by eating more sugar or grabbing another cup of coffee.

Start to notice these times. If it helps, keep a diary of what you eat and how it makes you feel—the full spectrum of emotions. Notice the headaches, the lightness, the energy, the tiredness, the rushes, the sensations, and make a point to do so objectively.

This doesn't mean you have to cut out foods, or that you should cut out things you enjoy eating. At this stage, it's more about cultivating awareness so that you can evaluate the evidence and make a conscious decision further down the line.

4. Learn the difference between cravings and needs

There is a very good reason that when we feel stressed, exhausted, have PMS (for women), or generally feel a bit "meh," we get the sugar cravings. The relationship between women and chocolate has become a stereotype, as has the Bridget Jones-like scene I described earlier in this book of the single 20- to 30-something woman comforting herself over a breakup, fight, or other negative life event, with a box of tissues, a box of chocolates, and a soppy movie.

There's truth in this cliché: eating lots of chocolate leaves us feeling good (for a short while, at least). That's because it's one of the Band-Aids we talked about earlier: it fills an emotional need, even just for a moment. Of course, once the chocolate is gone, it's gone (or we simply can't stomach any more), but the emotional need is still there. When we use something like chocolate to try to fulfill an emotional need, we also risk sacrificing our physical health.

Recognising that we're experiencing an emotional need can be challenging in the moment. Even though the root of the craving is an emotional need, the conscious thought we experience is "I want (or even need) cake." Underneath, we might feel lonely, rejected, disappointed, self-critical, or any of a range of challenging, uncomfortable feelings. What that translates to in our minds, though, is "I could really do with a biscuit right now."

Like all addictions, acting on the cravings is a block to our authentic selves, because it's like slapping a Band-Aid on a need. Satisfying the craving doesn't meet the need; it only covers it over until it presents itself again. And it *will* present itself again, because by trying to assuage an uncomfortable feeling with food, we're missing the emotional need entirely.

To stop this cycle in its tracks, start questioning the cravings. The answers won't be obvious immediately, but you can start digging around, pulling back the curtain and investigating what's really going on underneath the sugar pull.

Questions that might be helpful to consider include:

- *Why am I craving this particular thing?*

- *What happened immediately before I started craving it?*

- *How has my mood been today? What emotions have come up in particular?*

- *Has anything happened that has particularly stressed or upset me today?*

- *What self-critical thoughts have I had about myself today? Can I sense any connection between the critical thoughts I had and my desires for food?*

As you become more practiced at questioning your cravings, and at differentiating your cravings from your needs, you'll discover your own questions too. Keep a note of them, as they will deepen your insight into what's happening for you unconsciously around cravings and needs.

5. Get support

Like money and sex, eating—namely, eating habits—is one of those taboo topics that many people feel uncomfortable talking about. However, for that very reason it's important to get support from other people. Whether you have someone with whom you can explore your options, someone who is willing to discuss your exploration into cravings, needs, and how you can incorporate self-care into your food choices with you, or someone who is willing to join you on the journey, having one or more companions along the way to support, motivate, and provide you with insights will help your food-related self-care.

Why it works

Once we can identify which needs are underneath our cravings, we're in a much better position to do what we can to meet those needs. Instead of putting a Band-Aid over them, we can find ways to meet the underlying needs more fully with practices and behaviors that are not only more effective, but also better for our health and self-esteem.

15

REMEMBER TO BREATHE

———

Your breathing is your greatest friend. Return to it in all your troubles and you will find comfort and guidance.

—*Unknown*

Needs: Acceptance, closeness, compassion, love, nurturing, self-respect, security, stability, air, presence, space, awareness, celebration of life, consciousness, understanding

Our physical state has a huge impact on our emotional well-being. We talk about how physical tension can affect our emotional tension several times throughout this book, and this chapter focuses on another aspect of how our physical state can change our emotional state too:

Breathing

Let's start with a little test:

Set a timer for 30 seconds and start breathing rapid, shallow breaths, as you would if you were panicking about something or had just experienced a shock. If you start to feel dizzy, *please stop immediately*; otherwise, carry on for the full 30 seconds. Now notice how you feel physically. You might feel tense, slightly nauseated, the beginnings of a headache, even a touch of the jitters. Pay attention to how you feel emotionally. In most cases, you'll feel more anxious than you had felt before you started the exercise—perhaps you can feel a mild adrenalin rush making its way through your body.

Of course, nothing has happened in those 30 seconds to make you feel more anxious—except for the change in your breath. That's how powerful our breathing can be. Because it's something we do constantly, and because it's controlled by our lizard brains, we don't often even notice the quality of our breathing or how it might affect how we're feeling. This shows up at various times, for example, when we're concentrating on something or we're waiting for important news, and suddenly find we've been holding our breath. When it comes, we exhale deeply, breathing a sigh of relief and releasing not only the breath we'd been holding in anticipation, but usually pent up physical tension too.

Yes, much of our breathing is unconscious; therefore, we're not always aware of the ways in which it might be affecting how we feel. This can lead to a chicken and egg scenario, where we feel anxious or upset about something and mirror this emotion with a physical response. The physical response exacerbates our emotional reaction, which deepens the initial feeling even further.

The flip side of this is that we can also use our breath to reconnect with ourselves, our physical feelings, and our emotions. This idea contains one simple exercise that will help you do just that.

How it works

This suggestion comes in two parts: a practice you can use whenever you want to relieve tension and stress, and a practice you can use when you are feeling overwhelmed by uncomfortable or difficult emotions.

Part 1: Home Practice

Sit in a chair or lie down somewhere comfortable. Close your eyes and take five deep breaths, bringing your focus to your breath as much as possible. With your eyes still closed, breathe normally and bring your attention to the physical feelings around your body. Do you feel any tension? Is anything hurting? Are you tired?

When you arrive at areas that feel tense, take a deep breath and imagine you are breathing out the tension. Do this as many times as you need for each part of you that is holding on to some kind of energy or tension from your day.

Now bring the focus to your emotions. How are you feeling? Perhaps it's hard to identify what you're experiencing right now. That's OK. The more you come back to this practice, the easier it will be to connect to your emotions. If you can identify feelings, then that's great—stay with them. Shift your breathing so that you're taking in slow, deep breaths. These breaths need to be long enough to provide you with a sense of calm and stillness, yet not so long that, after a while, you're gasping for oxygen.

Breathing deeply, notice how your breath is affecting the way you feel. Perhaps you feel emotions like anxiety, hurt, or anger calming through your deep breathing. Perhaps they don't feel calmer, but you still feel able to sit with them and hold them without acting on them.

Stay here for as long as you want. You can return to this practice regularly to develop a deeper connection with your breath.

Part 2: Breathing in the Moment

This part of the suggestion is useful for times when you think you might be overwhelmed by what you're feeling. Overwhelm—particularly when it comes to uncomfortable or "negative" emotions—can leave us feeling frightened and helpless. When we're feeling overwhelmed, we're also far more likely to act out on our feelings than to sit and just experience them.

You can use your breath to take a step back from overwhelm by employing the practice described above. If you feel in danger of entering overwhelm, start breathing deeply and focus on where the physical tension lies in your body. Use your breath to let go of some of that tension, then turn your focus to your emotions. Continue taking long, deep breaths, noticing your feelings but not getting caught up in the stories behind them. Doing this helps you take a step back from being "in" your feelings, without repressing them. By paying attention to the emotion but not running away with the story, you can more easily observe and acknowledge your feelings without them controlling you.

Continue this process for as long as you need.

Why it works

The breathing routine described above can last for as much or as little time as you want. It's a useful way to get back in touch with yourself if you're feeling overwhelmed or are finding it hard to listen to what your body is telling you. It's also useful during periods when we might find it hard to connect to certain emotions. During those times, we often have a physical reaction, as well as the emotional response. Slowing our breathing, ensuring we're getting enough oxygen, and reducing the physical response to these feelings can help the feelings to become more manageable.

As I mentioned above, this process isn't the same as repressing these feelings (that isn't helpful). Instead, it's about learning to *self-soothe*. When we're in a situation of panic, feeling very exposed, or feeling overwhelmed, we are not in a place where we can make good decisions for ourselves. When we quiet the physical response to these feelings, we calm the emotions themselves, which helps us take steps to get our needs met in a healthy way (and reduces the chance that we'll take unhealthy steps to do so).

16

CONNECTION

Needs: Acceptance, affection, appreciation, belonging, cooperation, communication, closeness, community, companionship, compassion, consideration, consistency, empathy, inclusion, intimacy, integrity, love, mutuality, nurturing, respect, safety, security, stability, support, to know and be known, to see and be seen, to understand and be understood, trust, warmth, touch, authenticity, presence, meaning, growth, learning, participation, self-expression, stimulation, to matter

Connection is one of our basic human needs. It is absolutely necessary for our physical and mental health, and it has multiple positive effects and benefits on our overall well-being.

When we're stretched for time, and when other priorities get in the way, connecting with friends and family can start to feel like a luxury, even an obligation, rather than an activity that meets our need for connection. Instead of giving ourselves permission to meet this need, we start denying it. Instead of viewing it as it really is: a basic human need, we start viewing it as an optional indulgence. We prioritize other commitments and let our connections slip.

This in itself isn't a problem. It's something we've all experienced at one point or another. If it happens repeatedly, however, it can lead to a pattern that makes it harder for us to establish relationships and disrupts our long-term support system.

The pattern is most likely to occur when we start to feel shameful. Perhaps we've cancelled on someone more times than we feel comfortable, maybe we forgot to turn up to support a friend in need, perhaps we promised to return a phone call then realized two weeks later that we never did. Whatever the case, when our inner dialogue becomes critical, we are far less likely to be able to turn that ship around. Consequently, we avoid taking remedial action, the silence continues, and the longer it goes on, the harder it becomes to make the call, send the email or reach out. As we've already talked about in the introduction, shame-based action (or inaction) creates a vicious cycle. In this context, the cycle can leave us feeling very alone and bereft of support.

How it works

This suggestion is about making connection conscious. It involves making a decision to reach out to one or more important person(s) in your life each week and maintain the social system that is crucial to your health, happiness, and support.

I find it helpful to schedule this into my diary. Whether you use a task management program, or a calendar, set a recurring appointment or a to-do task for the same time each week, and carry it out. If you're not sure who to connect to, make a list of everyone you know with whom you want to maintain or develop your relationship. Choose at least one person from the list per week and stick to that commitment.

You can also use this scheduling method to rekindle old friendships or relationships. If you want to reconnect with people but haven't spoken for a while, make a list of people you want to get in touch with and commit to a time each week when you will reach out to an old friend or acquaintance.

Another process I have found useful for keeping in touch with people is a productivity tip from Merlin Mann called "Inbox Zero." This process is designed to help people stay on top of their emails, but applying it can improve our sense of connection too. I can easily let my emails pile up, unanswered and sometimes even unread, until the number is so overwhelming that I want to avoid the arduous task of clearing and responding to them. These might all be emails from important friends, people I enjoy talking to, and people I admire, but my inner taskmaster declares that I can only answer personal emails after everything else is done.

So I make getting to Inbox Zero a weekly task on my to-do list. As the name suggests, it requires clearing out all emails from your inbox. Some just need to be filed, others will require a more lengthy response. This is still a work in progress for me, but I know that sticking to my Inbox Zero routine as closely as possible not only keeps me organized, but also helps me stay in touch with the people who are most important to me.

Who do you want in your community?

The people with whom we interact, and the people we bring into our community determine whether or not we meet this need. In her book *Overcoming Underearning*,

Barbara Stanny talks about the different kinds of people that together create a supportive, understanding, and nurturing community.

According to Barbara, four kinds of supporters are important in your community.

1. **True Believers:** These are people who recognize your potential and celebrate even the smallest success. They are the ones who say "go for it" and are your community cheerleaders.

2. **Confidantes:** These are the people you turn to when you need a sounding board. They are the people you can talk to about your personal development, your quest to live an authentic life, and your challenges and successes along the way. They understand the steps you're taking to change and are there to support you through the highs and lows of your journey.

3. **Way Showers:** Way Showers are role models. They might be people you know directly or people you watch from a distance. People in this category are proof of authentic living. They say, "You can do it too; let me show you how."

4. **Messengers:** Messengers are information bringers. They are the connectors, the referrers, and the people that can provide you with leads that will further your authentic living. These are people who say, "I can help."

And then there are the **naysayers.** These are the people who are not supportive of your explorations into authenticity and behave like you need to conform to their expectations, ideals, and wishes. Naysayers will argue every which way against your authentic self. You can (usually, but not always) recognize people in this category by their use of emotive language, emotional blackmail, criticism, judgment, and blame.

Needless to say, the ideal community includes a minimal number of naysayers (if it contains naysayers at all) and an even spread of people who fit into the other four categories. It can be helpful to make a list of the people you know, specifying which category they fall under, so that you have a broader picture of how your community looks right now and where you might want to expand it.

Why it works

Connection is a basic human need and our connections with others help us in numerous ways.

Humans are pack animals. We have an evolutionary drive to be part of a community or tribe. Our ancestors depended on safety in numbers to survive. As children, we relied on other people to feed us, clothe us, and do everything for us in order to survive. Our brains are hard wired to be part of a community, so when we don't have a meaningful community around us, we suffer all kinds of physical and emotional effects.

Evolutionary drive aside, when we're part of a community we gain a more accurate perspective of ourselves. We can tell a lot about a person by how they relate to others, and the same is true for how we relate to others too. When we are connected to others, we also learn more about ourselves. Other people act as partial mirrors, giving us their explicit feedback (albeit framed by their own world view and experience) and communicating their experience of us through a series of verbal and nonverbal messages. Through our interactions with others, we gain a level of self-awareness and self-knowledge that we don't necessarily reach in isolation because we are interacting with other people who have their own frame of reference, own needs, and own way of relating to the world.

Lastly, connection to others exposes us to new ideas. It reveals contradictions in our way of thinking, creates new questions and opportunities, and we learn more about the world through other people's life experiences and wisdom. Connection with others reveals our potential, stimulates our creativity, and opens up a range of life possibilities that we wouldn't necessarily consider without that external perspective and feedback.

In short, contact with the right kind of people is fulfilling, rewarding, and eye opening, as well as challenging and uncomfortable at times too (personal growth doesn't usually happen without some discomfort). It offers us a variety of experiences and perspectives we can use to enrich our understanding of who we are and our own experience of the world.

17

H.A.L.T

Needs: Acceptance, compassion, empathy, nurturing, self-respect, stability, support, to know and be known, trust, air, food, connection, rest and sleep, water, presence, effectiveness, to matter

HALT is a well-known acronym within behavioral addiction theory. It describes four unmet needs that might leave us in a vulnerable state. Even though it originates from addiction treatment, HALT is a valuable principle when applied to everyday situations, addiction or no addiction, as it contains four very basic needs that we need to meet to be properly taking care of ourselves.

How it works

HALT stands for:

- Hungry
- Angry
- Lonely
- Tired

If you feel any of those things, HALT. Eat something healthy and wholesome, search for the unmet need under the anger and turn it into a request, call a friend you trust and with whom you can connect, go to sleep, or take a nap.

It sounds simple and it is: the trick lies in having a connection with our bodies and minds to be conscious of when we have one or more of the above needs, and to be conscious of what we can do to meet those unmet needs as fully as possible.

Why it works

When we experience any of the HALT feelings, we have basic physical and emotional needs that we aren't meeting. When we continue to leave those needs unmet, we're not empathizing with them. When we're not empathizing with our own needs, we won't be able to empathize with others. When we're not able to empathize with ourselves and others, communication breaks down. We're not showing up as our best selves in our relationship with ourselves, so we're not showing up as our best selves in our relationships with others either.

If we're experiencing one or more HALT feelings but carry on regardless, we are more likely to act out in our communication with others and turn to unhealthy coping mechanisms that Band-Aid these unmet needs.

The next time you experience any of the HALT feelings, stop and think before you do anything else: What can I do to meet this need right now?

Respecting your innate needs is one of the most fundamental and self-loving acts possible.

18

TIME CHARTS

Needs: Compassion, consideration, consistency, empathy, nurturing, self-respect, stability, support, to know and be known, rest/sleep, integrity, authenticity, presence, honesty, connection, play, joy, order, autonomy, choice, freedom, spontaneity, independence, space, awareness, clarity, celebration of life, consciousness, discovery, effectiveness, efficacy, growth, purpose, understanding

This suggestion is designed to help you become conscious about how you're spending your time. Quite often, we think we have our time management under control, yet find our days slipping away quickly without really knowing why.

Our time on this planet is finite, yet many of us are unaware of how we're really spending it. We use the phrase "I'm too busy" as an excuse but, at the same time, we might find it hard to identify why we're too busy to do the things we want to do. If we're not conscious of how we're spending our time right now, it's hard to make a conscious decision about how to spend our time in a way that better serves us.

Creating a time chart stops this cycle in its tracks and gives you back control over how you spend your precious time.

How it works

Part 1

Time: 20-30 minutes (plus some in-between tracking)

As I'll talk about in *Wall Your Time*, a common variation on Parkinson's Law states that a task expands to fill the time available. If we're faced with something we don't particularly want to do and spend time avoiding it by looking at Facebook, pairing our socks, or other suddenly very important tasks, we're letting the thing we don't really want to do take far more time and energy that it needs to.

Having been self-employed for several years, I know this all too well. Time and time again, I've found that if I have three hours to complete a piece of work, it will usually take three hours. If I have an hour to finish the same piece of work, I can usually do it in an hour. I also know that I'm capable of pottering around during the day—ostensibly working but not really working—having an "oh crap, it's already 4pm" moment, then working late into the evening.

If that sounds familiar, this suggestion is for you. Even if it doesn't sound familiar, I guarantee that you can create more space and time in your life by becoming conscious about what it is you actually spend your time on.

This starts by creating three charts: "Wishful Now", "Real Now", "Ideal Now".

A quick note about charts

I love making charts, lists and anything that helps me feel like I'm organizing my life and getting everything ship shape. I'm aware, though, that not everyone shares my chart lust. I use notebooks or spreadsheet software for this kind of exercise, but you can create your charts using whatever method you want.

I'm going to talk about my charts because that's what I know best, but you can draw a timeline, a treasure map, or whatever you want. The most important thing is that it makes sense and is meaningful to you. Keep reading to see why...

Back to the nows

So we're making three charts: "Wishful Now", "Real Now", and "Ideal Now".

I find it helpful to set out each day of the week in half-hour increments. First I block off fixed things like sleep, exercise time, and weekday lunch times. Then, I add in various work projects, recurring weekly appointments, like calls with friends, then everything else I can think of that I do during the week.

The first chart to create is "Wishful Now." The "Wishful Now" chart is how you *think* you spend your time.

For example, if anyone asked me "What time do you finish work?" I would answer "Oh, usually about 6pm."

Not so.

I *like* to think I finish work by six p.m., but what usually happens then is that I take my laptop from the bedroom, where I work during the day, into the living room ... where I carry on working.

It's important not to over think the "Wishful Now" chart. Even if you notice a big difference between your "Wishful Now" chart and the other charts you're about to create, that's perfectly fine. As you create each chart, you'll become more conscious of the differences between how you think you spend your time and how you really spend your time. At the moment, however, our focus is on noticing, not changing.

Once you've created your "Wishful Now" chart, you can move onto the "Real Now" chart. This is something that you won't be able to complete now (if you do, it's more a "Wishful Now" chart than a "Real Now" chart). To complete the "Real Now" chart, take your "Wishful Now" chart and, at different points during the week, compare what's on the chart with what's *actually* happening. This helps us separate out what we think we should be doing, from what we're doing in reality, which is the important first step.

Notice where your actions match those on the "Wishful Chart" and where they diverge. Use this information to create your "Real Now" chart: an accurate representation of how you're really spending your time.

The third chart is the "Ideal Now" chart. This is a chance to go hog wild and create your wildest fantasy *dream week*. If it doesn't look anything like your current week, remotely realistic, or in any way achievable, that's great! This chart is about throwing caution to the wind and thinking, "If I could spend my time in a way that met my needs, was aligned with my values and was as pleasurable as possible, what would that look like?" As you create your "Ideal Now" chart, pay special attention to self-care. It might not be something you automatically include, but an important part of incorporating self-care into our daily lives is to be conscious and make time for it.

Creating an "Ideal Now" chart can provoke some discomfort, especially when it's not very aligned with our current lives, or we have trouble visualizing what our ideal lives would look like. It can be hard to see that there's a big gap between where we are now and where we want to be. Equally, when we know that we want change, we're just not sure what *kind* of change we desire, we can end up feeling more frustrated than inspired. Even if you're struggling with these challenges (*especially* if you're struggling with these challenges) creating a version of the "Ideal Now" chart is so, so important, no matter how ridiculous the things on the chart might seem and no matter how unlikely it feels to come to fruition. Your wishes, dreams, and desires are important, and the first step to coming anywhere close to taking action on them is to give them a voice.

So there we have the three charts: two to create today ("Wishful Now" and "Ideal Now") and one to create piece by piece over the next week ("Real Now"). When you've spent as long as you want tracking your "Real Now" chart—a week is a helpful length of time—feel free to move on to part two.

Part 2

20-30 minutes

It's a week later, and you've been filling out your "Real Now" chart. Set aside 20 to 30 minutes just for yourself. Compare your "Real Now" chart with your "Wishful Now" chart and make a note of everything that doesn't tally between the two charts. Like I said before, this process isn't about judging or to trying to change anything right now, it's about noticing and becoming more awarer. As you compare the two charts, consider the following questions:

1. *What do you notice that's different?*

2. *What things are you spending more time on than you thought?*

3. *What things are you spending less time on that you thought?*

4. *Is there anything on your "Wishful Now" chart that you're sacrificing to make room for other things?*

5. *How do you feel noticing these differences?*

6. *What is your internal dialogue saying right now as you view the difference between your "Wishful Now" and your "Real Now" charts?*

Now take a look at your "Real Now" compared to your "Ideal Now". These might seem very far apart at the moment, and that's OK. The purpose of this suggestion is to raise awareness. Notice how you feel and what your internal dialogue is saying about any differences between "Real Now" and "Ideal Now". Then, answer the following question:

What one step do you think you could take today to bridge (or start bridging) the gap between the two charts?

Often, change is not the result of one giant action, but a series of small steps.

However fantastical your "Ideal Now" chart might appear, naming the first step today will bring you closer to making it a reality.

PART 4

Nurturing the Body

19

INTRODUCTION

Our bodies are our gardens to which our wills are gardeners.

—*William Shakespeare*

In this section, we're moving on to more short-term self-care practices. These are the practices that build on the long-term self-care foundation we've just covered. To make your self-care as effective as possible, address your most basic needs around sleep, exercise, food, and the other suggestions from the previous section before moving on.

This section focuses on our bodies. It contains suggestions that build on the foundation practices we've just covered and that will continue to influence our physical well-being. After this section we'll shift our focus to self-care for the mind, exploring suggestions that influence our mental and emotional well-being.

Inevitably, you'll experience some crossover between your physical and mental or emotional well-being because the two are intrinsically linked: our emotional needs and physical needs are deeply connected. Mental and emotional benefits will occur as a happy side effect, but the main beneficiary of the following suggestions is your complex, hard working, wonderful, physical self.

20

R-E-L-A-X

Needs: Compassion, consideration, empathy, self-respect, support, rest and sleep, ease, choice, space, freedom, consciousness

Relaxing is a deceptively simple-sounding suggestion. Most of us assume that relaxation is easy, when in reality it can be far harder than we imagine.

Making time to relax is a challenge in a world where so much value is placed on striving, achieving, doing, and aiming higher. From a young age, we're taught—both explicitly and implicitly—that "productive" is good and "unproductive" is bad.

When this perception is taken too far, we can end up feeling pressured to always be doing something more, being something bigger and working, working, working.

We lose sight of the power of relaxation, and we lose sight of the fact that relaxation in itself is productive. We need time to decompress, relax, and let go to regenerate, rejuvenate, and renew ourselves, our ideas, and our energy.

To the striving parts of us, relaxation might feel unproductive. But relaxation is *not* unproductive. It is absolutely crucial for both our mental well-being and physical health.

Of course, we all know how to relax. We know that meditation, yoga, walks, reading a good book, and sitting down in front of a good movie are all great ways to have some down time. But at the same time we don't know *how* to relax. As we're doing all the above, our minds still race through everything we should be doing, tasks to do afterwards, current projects, current conflicts, current disruptions. We have all the tools and methods for relaxation, but it's hard to get to a place where we let ourselves sink into relaxation and give ourselves over to nothing. It's a whole other challenge to just sit and *be*.

How it works

This bit is tricky: I wish I had a single, simple answer that solved this problem and provided the key to unlock relaxation for all.

But I don't. I know what works for me (focusing on my breath, doing meditation, consciously going through each part of my body and physically relaxing it, hot baths after a hectic day). However, I'm not you.

Part of your self-care challenge is to find what helps *you* relax. To notice when you feel relaxed (hopefully some of the suggestions in this book will help) and to make a note of the moment it happened, what you were doing immediately before, and what about the environment helped.

By observing and noticing, you can steadily compile your own bank of relaxation activities and figure out your own relaxation equation. You'll learn to recognize that you enjoy reading, but it's too mentally stimulating to be truly relaxing. You'll learn that hot baths aren't enough to truly switch you off, but submerging yourself in a steamy room for a few minutes does the job just fine.

Experiment, play around, and, most importantly, *relax*.

Why it works

When we're constantly focusing on mental anxiety, stress, and tension, we set ourselves up to feel more mental anxiety, stress, and tension in the future. When we carry physical symptoms of anxiety stress, and tension, we place undue strain on parts of our body that aren't meant to be strained. Joints, muscles, skeleton, and organs can all suffer as a result of this strain. Our quality of life goes down and, ultimately, so does its duration.

When we make enough time to truly relax and switch off, we feel calmer and more energized. We become more resilient and able to handle life's curveballs. Our physical selves are happier, we stop carrying around unreleased tension in various parts of our bodies. We give ourselves a chance to recover and reenergize, and we are better in touch with our ability to experience *what is* right now, in this moment.

21

YOGA

Needs: Acceptance, community, compassion, empathy, nurturing, self-respect, warmth, movement and exercise, presence, beauty, ease, harmony, space, awareness, celebration of life, challenge, competence, clarity, consciousness, discovery, growth, hope, learning, participation, purpose, self-expression, stimulation

Yoga is an activity that spans a large scale, from "how can someone physically do that?!" at one end, to restorative at the other. Some schools of yoga are full of serious woo woo. Other types of yoga, however, are excellent for improving your strength and flexibility, as well as relieving stored tension in your body. Having practiced yoga on and off for a number of years, I recently started doing a minimum of 30 minutes most days. This consistency has really opened my eyes to the hidden benefits of yoga: as well as the purely physical benefits, yoga is a valuable tool for connecting with our physical and emotional feelings and needs too.

Quick disclaimer: I'm not a yoga expert, and I strongly recommend you contact your physician or a local yoga teacher if you have any questions about whether a particular type of yoga would be suitable for you. Not all yoga is easy-breezy-breathe-deeply, and it is possible to injure yourself if you execute poses or movements incorrectly. I'm an advocate of safe, responsible yoga practice, and I'm not liable for any injuries, ailments, or otherwise you experience as a result of trying this. If you decide to incorporate yoga into your self-care routine, please take responsibility for your own health and safety. Listen to your body!

How it works

If you're new to yoga, I strongly recommend taking at least one class before trying anything at home on your own. Doing this will give you a much better idea of the correct way to do some of the more common yoga poses, which will benefit you later and help prevent injuries.

If you have previous experience with yoga, and you feel confident that you can experiment with poses without injuring yourself, there are a number of free or low-cost resources you can use to build up a regular yoga practice. Details of all these, and more self-care resources, are included in the resources page for this book at *www.becomingwhoyouare.net/fctt-resources.*

Why it works

As I mentioned in the introduction, yoga works on a number of levels. On a purely physical level, it's great for developing strength and flexibility, it improves your posture, and, over time, it improves your stamina too.

You're also likely to experience mental and emotional benefits from a regular yoga practice. For a start, you're taking care of your physical health, which inevitably affects your mental health. When you practice yoga regularly, you experience several lessons firsthand, which are transferable off the mat in our day-to-day life, too. For example, it teaches us that we're dealing with different challenges and distractions each day but the most important thing is to show up and do our best.

In addition, there's something very satisfying about finally mastering a pose you've been struggling with for weeks, even months, and charting your progress. At the same time, that progress can be slow. Yoga teaches us to be patient with ourselves, patient with our bodies, and to accept that each day will feel different. On the other hand, I've also discovered through yoga that I feel liberated when I'm sure I can't do something, then just take a deep breath and do it (maybe not in the most graceful or dignified manner, but still do it). The first time I saw "wild thing" pose, I was sure I couldn't do it. As I followed the teacher's instructions, however, I just flipped my dog and, well ... did it. And that was that.

In this way, yoga can teach us several things:

1. **When we build up things in our mind, we often create an impression of them as bigger, harder, or more challenging than they really are.** We convince ourselves that certain challenges are impossible and deny ourselves the chance to try to prove that belief wrong.

2. **When we open ourselves up to new possibilities, we are capable of more than we might currently imagine.**

3. **Wherever we are today is fine, and if that's totally different tomorrow, that's also fine.** We can't squeeze our bodies or our minds into contorted positions if we're not ready—that's just a reality. Therefore, we have a choice: we can gripe and moan

at ourselves for being unfit, inflexible, and having double the amount of muffin top compared to the sexy yoga pro in the video, or we can just accept these things. We can focus on the things we are doing and the fact that we're doing our best, and we can feel proud of where we're at.

22

LAUGHTER

Do something every day that is loving toward your body and gives you the opportunity to enjoy the sensations of your body.

—Golda Poretsky

Needs: Acceptance, appreciation, belonging, communication, closeness, community, companionship, compassion, inclusion, intimacy, mutuality, nurturing, to see and be seen, warmth, authenticity, presence, play, joy, humor, freedom, spontaneity, celebration of life, participation, self-expression, stimulation

"Laughter is the best medicine" is an overused phrase that provides little comfort to those in the throes of a challenging situation or emotional overwhelm.

Laughter is not the best medicine for all situations. In the context of an average day, however when we want to ride the crest of a natural high for a few minutes, it can work wonders for our physical and emotional well-being.

How it works

This one is simple:

Do something that makes you laugh.

It's that easy. Do what you need to do: talk to someone whose sense of humor leaves you in stitches, queue up some entertaining videos on YouTube, listen to a clip of other people laughing (that usually works). The source of your laughter doesn't have to be high-brow, intellectual, or even dignified.

It just needs to make you laugh.

I once attended a workshop where one of the exercises involved the "laughter lawnmower." We each had an imaginary lawnmower that was powered by our laughter. The aim of the exercise was to get the lawnmower started (bellowing "Mwahaha" while pulling the imaginary starter cord did the trick) and then mow our way around the room all the while keeping our lawnmowers revved up with our laughter.

It only took about ten to fifteen seconds before no one was forcing their laughter anymore—we were all in genuine hysterics, tears streaming down our faces, rolling our imaginary lawnmowers around the room.

To anyone else entering the room at that moment, we would have looked *insane*. But we didn't care: in the midst of this surreal shared experience, self-consciousness, and dignity flew out the window. We lost ourselves in uncontrollable laughter, and I remember it fondly as one of the funniest experiences of my life (I'm still giggling writing about the experience now).

As I said... it doesn't have to be dignified.

Why it works

As you might have gathered from the example above, we're not talking about a small chuckle here: we're talking a big, belly tears-rolling-down-our-faces laugh. True belly laughter is never forced; it wells up from deep inside, as long as you give it the chance.

This laughter isn't meant to be controlled, we're not meant to retain our dignity, we're certainly not meant to look cool while doing it. It's a natural expression of something inside us that is just waiting to get out.

Laughter is an emotional and physical release. It is an outpouring of emotion, and it relieves physical tension. Laughter sends a rush of endorphins around our bodies, temporarily altering our chemical makeup. Laughter is infectious, and it changes the way we experience the world.

So go ahead, and let yourself really laugh. Use a lawnmower if you have to.

Trust me, you'll feel better for it.

23

SAVASANA

Needs: Acceptance, closeness, compassion, empathy, intimacy, love, nurturing, self-respect, security, stability, rest, air, presence, peace, space, awareness, celebration of life, consciousness, understanding

Savasana (or "corpse pose") is the last yoga pose in any practice, and the most important yoga pose of them all. In some kinds of yoga, such as Bikram, you get a mini-Savasana halfway through as well, once you've finished the standing series of postures. Many yoga teachers say that all the bending, stretching and breathing involved in the yoga poses is a warm up. Savasana is when the magic really happens.

How it works

If you're not familiar with it, one form of Savasana (the form we'll talk about here) looks something like the following steps. Although it usually follows yoga, we're not going to do yoga today—not the bendy, stretchy kind anyway (unless you want to, of course). We're just going to do Savasana, because sometimes that's hard enough.

How to do Savasana:

Lie down.

Separate your heels until they are a few inches apart and relax your legs, letting your feet flop out to the side.

Bring your arms, palms facing upwards, about two inches away from the rest of your body.

Extend your neck, so that your chin is slightly tucked towards your chest (this should be comfortable—if it feels like you're stretching, you've gone too far).

Then, breathe.

Relax.

Focus on your breath.

Stay here for as long as you can (at least five to ten minutes).

That's it.

Why it works

That's it…. Except it's not it—that's just the beginning of the pose. There's no more physical movement involved, but our minds are busy, busy, busy with thoughts. Even when our body is still and relaxed, our minds are still working.

In Savasana, you bring it all back to the breath. As I once heard a yoga teacher explain it, in savasana:

"You are calmly active and actively calm."

Sometimes, people fall asleep—especially at the end of a yoga class. If possible, stay alert. Notice your thoughts popping up, tapping on the window of your mind, and bring your attention back to your breath.

Savasana is essentially a form of meditation. Like meditation, we're training our minds, developing an awareness of our physical and emotional feelings and focusing on *noticing* what's coming up, while resisting getting caught up in our mind's stories or judging what's happening.

I believe that when we start the day like this, we stand a good chance of taking that perceptive awareness forward:

Calmly active and actively calm.

24

PARTY LIKE IT'S 1999

Needs: Movement/exercise, authenticity, presence, play, joy, humor, freedom, spontaneity, celebration of life, participation, self-expression, stimulation

This suggestion is simple, and, most importantly, *fun*. It works as a pick-me-up, energizing your body and your mind. All you need is some kind of music player (MP3, phone, laptop, radio) and your enthusiasm. Headphones are optional, depending on the proximity of your neighbors.

How it works

Find a song that resonates—preferably one that is upbeat, but definitely one that resonates. Perhaps you like the beat, the lyrics speak to you, or it's the kind of tune that sticks around in your head for at least a month after each listen.

Plug your headphones in or play it out loud, turn up the volume, and get moving.

Sing, dance, do whatever you need to do. If you feel self-conscious about other people seeing or hearing you, close the curtains, look the door, and turn the music up louder.

Don't be afraid to work up a sweat, and stop as soon as it's not fun anymore.

And that's it. Like I said: simple, yet very, very effective.

Why it works

As it turns out, the doctors are probably wrong: exercise doesn't really have that much effect on our weight after all. What it does do, however, is provide us with numerous other positive side effects, including a brighter mood, more energy, and a better night's sleep. This self-care suggestion puts those benefits to good use—without the torturous resistance-provoking gym sessions. Win-win all round.

25

RELIEVING TENSION

The body says what words cannot.

—*Martha Graham*

Needs: Belonging, closeness, compassion, nurturing, self-respect, warmth, rest, peace, space, awareness, consciousness,

In *R-E-L-A-X*, we talked about how our bodies can store emotional tension as physical tension and that physically releasing tension from our bodies can help us release emotions too. This also works the other way around: when we're physically tense for any reason, we can take on this tension emotionally too (if you want to try this out, hunch your shoulders for as long as you can and see how you start feeling...). Besides potentially causing physical pain, which never helps our emotional well-being, the mere presence of physical tension can leave us feeling stressed. As I explained, it's a chicken and egg situation: our physical tension affects our emotional and mental tension just as much as our emotional or mental tension affects our physical tension.

With that in mind, this suggestion is going to look at how we can use the release of physical tension to create a sense of calm and relaxation in our minds too.

This exercise is something I've found especially useful since I discovered meditation. During my day-to-day life, any tension I'm feeling shows up in my shoulders, my jaw, and a frown line on my forehead, above the center point between my eyes. By the time I notice it's there, this tension has usually arrived, unpacked, and made itself at home. It can be caused by my emotions, my posture, and simply the fact that I sit at a computer for most of the day (in various locations that might or might not include a desk).

I first experienced this kind of relaxation method when reading *"The Mindful Way Through Depression,"* by Jon Kabat-Zinn (a highly valuable book that's beneficial for anyone to read). He calls it a "body scan." Below is a slightly modified version of this, designed to maximize the release of physical tension from our bodies.

How it works

To complete the body scan, either read and remember the paragraphs below or create a recording of yourself reading the process below aloud (if you do this, remember to leave enough silence so you can sufficiently focus on each body part). This scan works best if you're lying down, but sitting in a chair is also fine. Sit or lie comfortably (in Savasana pose—see the suggestion involving *Savasana* for details on what this looks like), with your legs slightly apart, feet falling out to the side, arms loose by your side, shoulders relaxed and palms facing upwards.

Close your eyes and bring your attention to your breathing. Don't change your breathing, simply focus on each breath, in and out.

A quick note about focus: If your thoughts drift off to anything else, whether it's what you're having for dinner, a looming deadline, another person, or feeling self-conscious, just bring them back to your breath or the relevant body part as soon as you notice. Don't get caught up in self-chatter about being "wrong" for getting distracted or worrying about your levels of focus. No matter how much we do this kind of exercise, we will always have days when it feels near impossible to focus (even when we're not sure why). There's nothing wrong with this at all, it's simply something else to be aware of.

So, back to the breathing. After a few breaths, begin the body scan. For each part of the scan, focus your attention on that body part.

Starting with your feet, tense the muscles as much as you can and hold this for a few seconds. Then release completely, letting the muscles relax. Tense them again and release again two times, so that you cycle through this tense and release pattern three times in total.

Shift your attention to your calves and lower legs, and repeat the same cycle. Tense, relax. Tense, relax. Tense, relax.

Shift your attention to your thighs and repeat.

Work your way up through your body, focusing on your abdomen, then your chest, then your shoulders, your upper arms, your lower arms, your hands, your neck, your jaw, then finally your face and scalp (very important—often we hold lots of tension here without even realizing it). With each part, tense as much as you can, then relax as much as you can three times. At the end, you can slip in to a meditation, focusing on your breathing and enjoying your relaxation.

(And yes, if you want to take a nap, that's more than OK too.)

Why it works

We all have places in which we tend to carry around physical tension. When the tension enters these typical hot spots, we can become so accustomed to it that when we try to "relax," we don't even know what that feels like anymore ("I *am* relaxed," I've said in the past, with my shoulders hunched up to my ears). We might find it difficult to connect with that part of our body and find it hard to release the tension we're holding, or we simply forget what "relaxed" feels like.

By tensing first, we not only introduce movement into a specific part of the body, but we also focus our attention on it and therefore reconnect with how it feels, and how we can control our muscles there. That put us in a much better position to relax further and let the tension go.

Other thoughts

We have a *lot* of muscles in our body, which means there's much potential for us to carry around tension. With each tense and release cycle, try tensing the body part in focus in a different way. For example, try scrunching your hands or feet, the first time, then try flexing them as much as you physically can the next time. The third time, follow your gut and go with what feels good.

Introducing some variety in the movement means you're more likely to get to those hard-to-reach areas. It also allows you to give tense muscles even more of a stretching, leaving them more able to relax afterwards.

26

CREATE A SELF-CARE KIT

Needs: Acceptance, affection, appreciation, closeness, compassion, consideration, consistency, empathy, intimacy, love, nurturing, self-respect, support, authenticity, presence, play, peace, autonomy, space, awareness, growth, self-expression, to matter

This suggestion is about going to the spa.

Not a *spa* spa mind you: this suggestion is about finding a balance that enables us to dedicate time to our pleasure, relaxation and well-being without compromising other needs, such as our need to be able to buy groceries or feel financially secure.

In that way, think of it more as a metaphorical spa.

As we've already discussed, self-care is not about taking yourself out for manicures, Columbian waxes, or whatever the latest fashion trend is at the time of reading. It's about meeting your needs. If you're on a budget or short of time, you're not going to meet your needs by buying expensive treatments or taking several hours you don't have out of your day—in fact, doing this will probably stress you out even more.

Having said that, there's a reason why plenty of people opt for professional treatments and attention, over a purely aesthetic motive: *showing your body some TLC feels good*. It is certainly one form of self-care, it's just that we need to find a way to treat our bodies well without compromising any other needs we have that are jostling for attention alongside.

As I said in the introduction, self-care isn't so much about what we "do," it's about meeting our needs.

So we might not be able to *go* to a fancy spa (without leaving one or more of our other needs wanting, anyway) but we can certainly try to recreate the *feeling* of going to a fancy spa.

One way to do this is to create a "self-care kit."

How it works

The self-care kit is a collection of items that provoke your desired feelings.

This is a very personal experience, so I'm not going to provide a prescriptive list for what should go in your self-care kit.

Instead, the first step is to work out what your desired feelings are: what is it you would like to feel or experience after using your self-care kit?

This might include feeling:

Safe

Nurtured

Held

Warm

Relaxed

Rejuvenated

Replenished

Whole

Connected

Compassionate

Self-accepting

Understanding

Rested

Or any other words that are meaningful to you.

The next step is to translate these feelings into actions. What can you do that will help you get to these feelings and experiences?

Here are a few suggestions to get you started:

Meditate

Gentle yoga

Face mask

Long, hot bath

Incense

Quotes or affirmations

Special music

A good book

A journal

A scented candle

Your own personal self-care kit might contain all of these, or it might contain none of them. As I said, this is a personal experience, so spend time thinking about how you can recreate your desired feelings with simple everyday items and activities.

Once you have a few ideas about the kinds of things you might want in your self-care kit, start compiling it. Begin simply, and test each individual item out for its effectiveness before adding the next. Sometimes, we think a certain item or activity is going to provoke certain feelings, but it doesn't. We might expect it to be relaxing and enjoyable, whereas in reality we find it uncomfortable and distracting. Equally, we might experience one activity or item in our kits very differently to how we imagined.

There's no rush: start small and build your kit over a period of several weeks or months. Schedule time to use your self-care kit and commit to that scheduled time. Whether it's fifteen minutes when you first get up, or you set aside a whole evening, *dedicate time*. Listen to how your self-care kit leaves you feeling, and listen to what your gut tells you to add or remove to enhance it and make it more effective at meeting your needs.

Why it works

Like the Mini-Retreat suggestion in the next section, the self-care kit is tailored specifically to you and executed on your terms. You're in complete control over how much time and money you spend on your experience, as well as when you choose to use your kit. This allows you to experience your desired feelings, set aside time to reconnect with yourself and give your body some TLC, without denying or ignoring other needs you might have, for example a need for financial stability.

Other thoughts

As you're probably aware, it's possible to spend a lot of time and money on so-called self-care items without even setting foot in a spa.

If you're concerned that engaging with this suggestion might provoke your money gremlins and inner critic, keep them at bay by setting some boundaries. This might take the form of a monthly self-care budget, a limit on the number of items you have in your kit, a limit for how much to spend on each item in your self-care kit, or all the above (on a practical note: remember that some items might cost more, but will last longer or indefinitely than other items that cost less).

Be as generous as you can be with your budget—remember there's nothing wrong with spending money on yourself—while still keeping your other needs in mind.

PART 5

Nurturing the Mind

27

INTRODUCTION

By your thoughts you are daily, even hourly, building your life; you are carving your destiny.

—*Ruth Barrick Golden*

The suggestions in this section focus on nurturing the mind. These are suggestions you can use to meet your physical and mental needs. They enable you to offer care and attention to this aspect of your well-being.

As with the previous section, how you use the suggestions in this section is up to you. Read all the suggestions through to begin with, then go back and start with the ones that resonate with you the most. Start by trying as many suggestions as you can. You might find that some suggestions don't sound that appealing initially but impact you right where you need them to.

Play around, be flexible, and most of all, enjoy.

28

CREATE A MINI-RETREAT

Needs: Acceptance, affection, appreciation, compassion, consideration, empathy, inclusion, intimacy, love, nurturing, self-respect, support, to understand and be understood, movement/exercise, rest/sleep, safety, touch, authenticity, presence, peace, inspiration, autonomy, space, celebration of life, clarity, discovery, growth, hope, learning, mourning, self-expression, stimulation, to matter

This suggestion follows on from the last (*Create a Self-Care Kit*): it's a way of going to the spa, without stepping foot in a spa.

I love the idea of going on a retreat. At the time of writing, it isn't something I've done, but I've been sorely tempted in the past and it's definitely on my "experiences" bucket list. At the same time, I know that it's not the retreat itself that part of me longs for, it's the *feelings* and *sensations* involved in that experience. In the initial chapters of this book, we explored how self-care is not about *what* you do, but about the *intention* behind it and the feelings that experience invokes.

This suggestion is about taking that principle and applying it to something that, conventionally, can be a big time and financial investment—like a retreat.

Here, you're going to discover how you can recreate the essence of your desired retreat in a way that works for you and your other needs too.

While you are totally free to go on a professional retreat (we can certainly benefit from a change of scene and time dedicated to self-care and reflection), the home mini-retreat is an option that provides a happy medium. Through this kind of activity, we can experience the desired feelings we seek, without having to spend time and money we're not ready to spend or sacrifice other important commitments and needs in the process.

How it works

As the name suggests, the home mini-retreat is something you can do from the comfort of your own home.

These retreats are ideal if you don't want to spend much time or money. They give you complete control over how long you spend, how much you spend, and what you do. Your home mini-retreat could be an hour lying on a bed, listening to music, or involve activities like yoga, hot bubble baths, and home beauty treatments.

As I mentioned in the introduction, the main aim of the retreat is to set an *intention*. What needs are you trying to meet with your retreat? What do you feel has been lacking in your life, and what are you yearning for? If you are aware of these things while you plan and prepare for your retreat, you are far more likely to be able to meet your needs.

Example retreat

Let's say that one of your burning ambitions is to go on a yoga retreat. It's been on your bucket list for a while, but the financial commitment of the retreat, the accommodation, and the transport, not to mention the time away from work, family, etc., feels too much.

To get the benefits of a yoga retreat, you don't need to go to Costa Rica or spend ten days in a Thai jungle. Simply work out an intention for the retreat, and you can go about creating it in your own home. Take a look at the itineraries of several yoga retreats you would consider attending, time and cost aside. Then, think or write down the elements you particularly like. Is it the two yoga sessions a day? The meditation time? The device and electronics-free time for reading or journaling? The vegan food? The opportunity to go hiking or learn local crafts?

Once you have this list, it's time to get creative. How can you recreate this in a way that meets your current needs?

For example, could you take a day where you can start with a yoga session, take a walk in the country, make time for meditation, prepare a healthy lunch, spend the afternoon reading, and then enjoy another yoga session in the evening? Could you spend a single afternoon in gentle yoga practice and meditation, followed by a nourishing meal with friends?

This is just one example of how you could use your retreat time. You don't have to take a day or even an afternoon; you can adjust the amount of time you spend depending on your needs, plus any other constraints or opportunities you might have.

Why it works

A home mini-retreat is less about what you *do* and more about what you want to get from it. As I said in the introduction, any self-care activity is a lot more effective if you can identify an intention behind it, and home mini-retreats are no exception.

When planning a mini-retreat, the important thing is to focus on the feelings and experience you want (just like when you're planning your self-care kit). Once you know what you want the *effect* of your home mini-retreat to be, you're in a much better position to plan how to create those feelings.

Other thoughts

For more retreat-based ideas and suggestions, I recommend *Woman's Retreat Book,* by Jennifer Louden (HarperOne, 2005). It's packed with thought-provoking practices that provide inspiration for your own at-home retreat.

29

TREAT LIST

Needs: Affection, appreciation, compassion, consideration, consistency, love, nurturing, self-respect, authenticity, play, peace, autonomy, celebration of life, to matter

Although I want to distance us from the idea that self-care is all about treating yourself (it's not—remember: *self-care is healthcare*), allowing yourself pleasures can certainly be part of your self-care routine. As a small caveat to this suggestion, I want to repeat what I said earlier in this book about making sure you've met your basic needs, like those from *Part 3*, before moving on to suggestions like the one below.

This is because, whether we're conscious of it or not, we're always striving to meet our needs. If we don't do this consciously, we start to do it unconsciously. That means that if you have unmet needs when engaging in this suggestion, you're going to be using the treats as a Band-Aid for deeper needs. As we've already talked about, this Band-Aid effect will provide temporary release, but it won't meet the need in the long term. It could also lead you to act in a way that compromises your other needs, for example spending time and money that you need for other essential items or activities. To get the most out of this suggestion, focus on meeting your physical and emotional needs first, and you'll find maximum pleasure and fulfillment in the idea below.

How it works

The first step is to start keeping a "someday" list of things you think it would be pleasurable to do, own, experience, or try. This might include a book you want to read, a long walk you want to do, a certain place you want to visit, sleeping in, and so on. You don't need many items on the list to begin with, as you can keep adding to it as and when ideas come to you.

When the time feels right, start scheduling treats for yourself into your calendar. Try to set up some kind of regularity, at a frequency that feels comfortable, whether that's daily, weekly, or monthly. I enjoy thinking about my list of "someday" treats on Fridays, as it feels like a helpful transition from the workweek into the weekend.

Why it works

A treat list involves items or activities that feel special. They are the kind of things that if we engaged in them on a daily basis would stop being special (and, in my case, potentially lead to an expensive book-buying habit) but in moderation they are enjoyable, fulfilling, and feel nurturing.

Sometimes, it feels good to have something to look forward to. I love my "job," but it still entails tasks I don't enjoy or that push me outside my comfort zone. At the end of some Monday to Friday weeks, I feel good about having taken up the challenges of the past five days, but I also look forward to giving myself a treat—whether that's a Starbucks, dedicated reading time, an episode of my favorite TV show, a book from my wish list, or any number of other things I enjoy. I find it motivating to know that these things are here at the end of the week, and it marks the transition into the free time of the weekend.

30

WRITE A LETTER TO YOUR FUTURE SELF

Needs: Acceptance, affection, appreciation, communication, connection, companionship, compassion, consideration, empathy, love, nurturing, self-respect, honesty, joy, harmony, meaning, celebration of life, consciousness, creativity, discovery, efficacy, effectiveness, growth, hope, learning, self-expression, to matter, understanding

Writing a letter to our past selves is an effective self-therapy tool that can help us process our histories, specific events, the emotional consequences, and develop our empathy and acceptance of our past selves. Here, we're going to turn this idea around and write a letter to ourselves *in the future*.

How it works

Writing effective letters to our future selves requires a pen, paper, and envelope (or a computer), plus a willingness to introspect and identify what we love and appreciate about ourselves. When you do this, it's helpful to think of your "best self"—why would you describe that version of yourself as your best self, and what do you love about that self in particular?

To start, make a list of all the qualities you love about yourself. *Do not skip this step.* It might feel uncomfortable and rather like writing a resume at first, but sit with that discomfort and try to focus on what you like about yourself as a person, as opposed to what you've achieved. If it feels really uncomfortable, set a timer for twenty minutes. At the end of the twenty minutes, you can get up and walk away from your list. While that timer is running, however, you're going to sit, think about and write down the things that make you "you," and why you appreciate and enjoy them.

When it comes to writing the letter, start by addressing yourself. For me, this would look like: "Dear Hannah,".

Then, continue to write the most honestly and genuinely gushing message you *have ever written to anyone*. I don't mean ass kissing—that won't come across as convincing or genuine. Instead, I'm talking about an authentic and vulnerable expression of your love. If the idea of writing a love letter to yourself weirds you out (as it did me at first), pretend that you're someone else, writing a letter to [your name here]. Talk about all the great, wonderful, lovable, admirable, and attractive qualities you have, and don't hold back. This letter is for you only, so don't worry about what other people would think if they read it—it's none of their business.

When you're done, seal it in an envelope or save it to your hard drive and wait.

At this point, you have a choice. You can either wait for an unspecified point in the future until you need a pick-me-up or a way to press the reset button on your inner critic.

Alternatively, you can specify a date, writing it on the front of the envelope or storing it on your hard drive marked "To open: [date here]." This is especially useful if you know you have a challenging time coming up that is going to stretch you emotionally or push you outside your comfort zone. If you know there's a specific time in the future (near or distant) when you're going to need support, name that date and store the letter until then.

Why it works

Writing a letter to yourself in the future enhances your self-care in two ways:

1. It encourages you to focus on the positive aspects of yourself and strengthens your inner "nurturing voice."

2. It gives you a tool for self-soothing and self-comforting at a time when you need it the most. When we're faced with situations that heighten our emotions and provoke overwhelm, it can be challenging for us to bring ourselves back to a place of internal stability and comfort, where we feel able to cope with what life throws at us. Whether you write the letter with a specific date in mind, or simply save it until you feel you need support, it acts as an external source of reassurance, validation and strength. Even though you were the one who wrote the letter, after enough time passes, you'll have enough distance from your words so that they feel fresh during a time of need.

Other thoughts

If you're composing your letter digitally, make use of available technology. For example, Gmail users can use an app called Boomerang and schedule their letters to land in their inboxes on a certain date.

31

CREATE UNPLANNED TIME

_____

Needs: Connection, Support, trust, authenticity, integrity, presence, honesty, play, peace, autonomy, choice, freedom, independence, space, spontaneity, creativity, discovery, growth, learning, purpose, self-expression, understanding

When was the last time you consciously portioned off part of your day as "unplanned time"?

Probably rarely, if ever.

Unplanned time is a hallmark of early childhood that fades in adulthood (perhaps we regain it again in retirement, but not always). When this happens, we can lose touch with a vital part of ourselves and our instincts. We spend so much time running around from activity to activity, commitment to commitment, and deadline to deadline, that we forget what it feels like to just *be*. In the days before music lessons, sports games, school, and other activities took over, every day was unplanned—we simply listened to our needs, did what we could to meet them, and paid attention to developing our interests in the moment.

Regaining our penchant for unplanned time is challenging. The very act of planning and executing unplanned time goes against many core beliefs about the virtues of productivity and what it means to be a "successful" or even "worthy" person. In a world where we place much value (and, internally, pride) on being busy, in demand, and juggling several balls at once, unplanned time gets squeezed out (just like relaxation) in favor of high achieving and our desire to feel valuable.

Now, we're going to get it back.

How it works

Unplanned time can seem very simple—after all, the whole point of unplanned time is that you *don't* plan anything to do.

In reality, however, planning unplanned time can be a challenge. First, it's ideal if you can find at least thirty minutes where you won't be disturbed. By anyone. You'll also make the most out of your time if you can turn off your phone, laptop, and any other device through which you are contactable. Not silent, not airplane mode, not a here's-another-way-I-can-get-around-turning-it-off substitute. Completely turn it off.

Next, unplanned time works best if you can make sure you're in a position where you have options. For example, if you want to meditate, you have the resources to do so. Alternatively, if you want to try your hand at painting, you can also do that fairly easily. This aspect of unplanned time isn't so easy to prepare, as, again, the whole point of unplanned time is that you don't plan it. Notice what what activities you're drawn to the first few times, and you'll be in a better position to "prepare" for what might come up in future unplanned sessions.

When it comes to "living" the unplanned time, turn everything off, and wait. Do not engage with your to-do list and set aside any thoughts that come up about what you *should* be doing with the time for later. Instead, notice what comes up and what your heart truly desires to do with the temporal space you've created.

What do you truly want to do with your time?

What do you desire to feel during this time?

What possibilities is your mind dreaming up during this time?

The first time you try this, simply sit and listen to the urges that come up. What do they tell you about the way you currently use your time? For example, do you keep feeling the need to do work or personal tasks? Do you feel like you should be doing something "productive" with your time?

The first time these feelings come up, don't act on them. Instead, notice them, observe them, even try having a dialogue with yourself about them.

The more you practice allowing yourself unplanned time, the more authentically you will start living the time.

Why it works

Unplanned time takes us back to our roots: spending our time how we *want to*, not how we feel we should. Once we've tried living unplanned time a few times, we might still feel the need to be doing "busy" or "productive" things. Slowly but surely, however, we'll also hear a growing voice that tells us what we really want to be doing with that time. What it says might surprise us, might feel alien, and might take some getting used to, but that voice will be more valuable to us than we might currently realize.

So unplanned time helps us become accustomed to parts of our internal dialogue—the voices that tell us what we should be doing and those that tell us what, deep down, we want to be doing.

It opens us up to new, exciting, even daring possibilities that we wouldn't have considered before. Once the busywork voices take a back seat, what comes up? What does our authentic self say about how we really want to be spending our time?

Living unplanned time—true unplanned time—helps deactivate the conditioned "you" and starts to reactivate the authentic "you" buried underneath.

Other Thoughts

Out of all the suggestions in this book, this one is potentially the hardest, so go easy on yourself. The first time you live your unplanned time, it will probably feel gut-wrenchingly awkward and uncomfortable. You might feel twitchy, disoriented, and little mad. Learning how to live unplanned time again is like exercising a muscle that we haven't used for 10, 20, 30 years, or more.

Please start with small amounts of time and get used to sitting with those uncomfortable feelings. They will pass the more you practice living unplanned time. Remember that this is something we used to do *all the time* when we were younger—it's the way we lived back then. Let's get some of that freedom and authenticity back.

32

NONVIOLENT COMMUNICATION

Being extremely honest with oneself is a good exercise.

—*Sigmund Freud*

Needs: Connection, acceptance, affection, appreciation, belonging, cooperation, communication, closeness, compassion, consideration, empathy, intimacy, mutuality, nurturing, respect, security, support, to know and be known, to see and be seen, to understand and be understood, trust, warmth, honesty, authenticity, integrity, presence, peace, equality, harmony, order, independence, space, awareness, consciousness, efficacy, effectiveness, growth, learning, participation, self-expression, stimulation, understanding

Nonviolent communication (NVC) is a tool that improves our communication with ourselves and with others. I dedicated a whole chapter to it in my last book, *The Ultimate Guide to Journaling* (2012), as it's an effective framework for looking at our internal dialogue when journaling. While I don't necessarily agree with everything the founder, Marshall Rosenberg, talks about, I have much appreciation for the way NVC mixes self-awareness with self-compassion and constructive communication skills.

If you're new to the idea of nonviolent communication, I highly recommend reading or listening to the book *Nonviolent Communication* (Puddledancer Press, 2003), by Marshall Rosenberg. This is available from major book retailers and on Spotify, where (at the time of writing), you can stream the audiobook for free. You can find numerous spin-off books and workbooks about NVC on websites like Amazon and on the Center for Nonviolent Communication website. On the NVC website, you can also find useful resources, including a list of feelings and a list of needs.

How it works

In a nutshell, NVC consists of three basic tenets:

1. Empathy for ourselves

2. Empathy for others

3. An honest expression of our feelings and needs

Beyond these three pillars, NVC also focuses on the differences between observing versus evaluating, feeling versus thinking, and expressing feelings versus expressing judgments. The framework and skills contained within NVC encourage us to be aware of our human needs and emotions and to express them in a way that is clear and genuine. The approach emphasizes personal responsibility, cooperation and collaboration, rather than demanding, manipulative, or shaming behavior in our relationships.

Within the NVC movement, the focus is on how we relate to other people. However, the same principles and framework also apply to how we relate to ourselves.

The first step in shifting our internal dialogue towards one that is more caring and compassionate involves *awareness* and *acceptance*. We need to be aware of what our feelings and needs are, and accept them, before we can take steps to meet them.

Journaling is one tool that can help us get back in touch with our feelings and needs, therapy is another. We can also make it a routine: set reminders or alarms for specific times of the day and, when they sound, ask yourself: "How am I feeling right now? What do I need right now?" When I started asking myself these questions, I struggled to identify the answers. I found the lists of feelings and needs on the CNVC website I mentioned above invaluable for helping me get back in touch with my emotions and identifying my unmet needs.

We can also improve our awareness by noticing our default responses and reactions to other people. When people ask you questions about your preferences, pay attention to how you respond. Often, we answer with a default response based on our conditioning and the dynamics that exist in our relationships with that particular person, among other things.

Our truly authentic answers, however, might be different. One of the biggest challenges involved in reconnecting with our feelings and needs is the conflict between how we feel we *should* be and how we really are.

Because of this, and because we might simply be out of practice, reconnecting with our needs can take time. Once we become more aware of them, however, and more accepting of them within ourselves, we're in a much better position to take action to meet our unmet needs and to communicate our feelings and needs to other people.

Why it works

So how does NVC aid our self-care?

As we talked about in the introduction, the majority of our self-care revolves around our internal processes, rather than external influences.

Self-care happens from the inside out. Even more important than how we communicate, negotiate, and express our feelings and needs to others is how we communicate, negotiate, and express our feelings and needs to *ourselves*.

An crucial part of self-care involves taking responsibility for our own needs and doing what we can to meet them. Our compassion and empathy for our own feelings and needs mirrors our compassion and empathy in our relationships. We cannot be truly empathic and compassionate with other people until we have developed empathy and compassion with ourselves first.

So as you can start to see, getting to grips with the NVC has a number of positive benefits:

1. We develop a more compassionate and understanding relationship with ourselves. We're far more likely to feel *happy and content*. After all, do you feel freer and more positive when spending time with people who are accepting, loving, and supporting, or those who criticize your appearance, question your life decisions, and constantly second-guess you?

2. We develop more intimate and fulfilling relationships with the important people around us. When we're more able to empathize with ourselves, we're more able to empathize with them. In other words, we're more able to show up as the best version of ourselves in relation to them: actively listening, actively expressing our needs and preferences, and actively empathizing both with ourselves and with them.

3. We develop our sense of self-responsibility. NVC emphasizes that *we are responsible for meeting our own needs*. Other people cannot meet our needs for us. No

one will care more about our well-being than we do, so if it's going to happen, we have to make it happen.

So here's a start:

What are you needing right now?

33

QUOTE BANK

Needs: Connection, communication, companionship, compassion, empathy, self-respect, support, to know and be known, to see and be seen, to understand and be understood, presence, peace, inspiration, awareness, clarity, consciousness, creativity, efficacy, effectiveness, growth, hope, learning, stimulation, understanding

The idea of a quote bank is similar to the *Affirmations* we'll talk about later in this section; after all, affirmations and quotes are both thought provoking, memorable, and meaningful statements.

A quote banks—as the name suggests—is a collection of quotes that have personal meaning for you. They might be relatable, inspiring, thought-provoking, or grounding.

Whatever their significance, quotes are a powerful way of reconnecting with aspects of ourselves that might get lost in day-to-day life, either because of our self-beliefs, because of our surrounding environment, or both. Aspects we might lose touch with could include our self-confidence, our connection with our needs, our burning ambitions or dreams, our willingness to step out of our comfort zone, and more.

The quotes in our quote banks function as metaphorical lighthouses, guiding us back to our desired purpose, feelings and guiding us back to ourselves.

How it works

Creating a quote bank is simple. Take a notebook, create a collection of index cards or create a new file on your computer. Think about quotes you have heard or seen that resonated with you and felt meaningful. If you can't remember the exact quote, google a few words to see what comes up.

If you're using index cards or collating the quotes digitally, try categorizing them by emotion, situation, or purpose so you can easily reference them in times of need.

Alternatively, you can leave the cards around your home and work, in places you know you'll use them. This might include your desk, your computer, your nightstand, and anywhere else you think is relevant.

Why it works

Creating quotes for your environment is especially useful if you're trying to break certain habits or patterns, or encourage new behaviors. For example, if you're trying to overcome a pattern of eating when you feel bored, stressed, or upset, place a quote next to your fridge (or the most tempting cupboard) that will help you reconnect with your nurturing self and encourage you to self-soothe, rather than turning to food.

Essentially, a quote bank can be whatever you want it to be. Use your quotes for inspiration, comfort, motivation, discipline—or all the above. People share their wisdom to help others, so make their wisdom work for you.

34

JOURNALING

There are days I drop words of comfort on myself like falling leaves and remember that it is enough to be taken care of by my self.

—Brian Andreas

Needs: Acceptance, appreciation, closeness, companionship, compassion, empathy, intimacy, nurturing, self-respect, safety, security, support, to know and be known, to see and be seen, to understand and be understood, honesty, authenticity, integrity, space, awareness, meaning, clarity, consciousness, creativity, discovery, growth, hope, learning, mourning, self-expression, stimulation, understanding

Journaling is one of the most effective self-therapy tools around, and it doesn't cost a thing. You don't even have to buy a notebook: if you'd rather keep your notes online, you can use one of the many websites specifically dedicated to journaling, or simply store plain documents in a cloud storage service like Google Drive.

As a practice, journaling is totally flexible and you have many different techniques to choose from. This means it's possible to start up a regular journaling practice even when you don't feel like you have much time to spend on self-care activities.

How it works

One of the benefits of journaling is that there is no right or wrong way to do it, and there are plenty of different suggestions and techniques you can use to explore your thoughts and feelings (you can find over 100 suggestions and prompts in my book, *The Ultimate Guide to Journaling*).

If you're new to the idea of journaling, try starting with a practice called "morning pages." This is an exercise from *The Artist's Way* (Putnam, 2002), by Julia Cameron that involves writing three pages (or about 750 words on a computer) of longhand each morning before you do anything else. These 750 words are supposed to be stream-of-consciousness, so write or type absolutely anything that comes into your head. Even if your mind goes blank and you can't think of anything to write about, writing "I can't think of anything to write about," is perfectly fine. The main thing is that you don't stop writing until you get to 750 words. (If 750 words feels too long to start with, try starting at 500 and increasing. Trust me—you *can* do 500 if you're willing to sit with the discomfort and get those words out.)

Other journaling practices you might enjoy include keeping a gratitude journal of ten to twenty things each day that you feel grateful for, starting a have-done list, containing all the things you've accomplished that day, or choosing a word and riffing on that theme for as long as your mind churns out related or associated words, phrases, and ideas.

The exact techniques and exercises you use don't particularly matter. What's most important is that you are dedicating a certain amount of time to exploring your thoughts and feelings each day or each week.

Why it works

Journaling encourages us to consciously explore our private thoughts and feelings. It is helpful for resolving internal conflicts, transitioning through life changes, working on our relationships with others, fostering a kinder internal dialogue, and much, much more.

The act of journaling itself is helpful, but what I call "retrospecting"—looking back at our previous journaling entries—can also shed new light on situations, people, and ourselves in the past. Making time to retrospect on a regular basis can open our eyes to new insights—and, consequently, self-awareness—that we wouldn't have otherwise had.

For more information about various journaling tools you can use to make your practice as effective as possible, take a look at the resources page for this book (*www.becomingwhoyouare.net/fctt-resources*).

35

CREATE SOMETHING

Needs: Connection, to know and be known, to see and be seen, authenticity, presence, play, joy, beauty, inspiration, freedom, spontaneity, celebration of life, challenge, competence, contribution, creativity, efficacy, effectiveness, growth, learning, participation, purpose, self-expression, stimulation

Creativity is an attribute that many people desire to have, yet so many believe they don't. The topic of creativity itself is far more emotive than it deserves. Too often, when we endeavor to do something creative (especially when we're a beginner), we are caught up in our own ideals and self-dialogue about perfectionism, comparison to others, and fear of mediocrity.

When we're in that place, it's very hard to just let ourselves create, whatever the consequences.

The truth is that *we are all naturally creative*. The things we create don't define us as people, but we do pour a lot of ourselves into our creative endeavors, so it can *feel* like they define us. There's a deep vulnerability in both surveying our handiwork and showing it to other people, to be judged as they so wish. When people do judge something we've created, it's not hard to feel like they are judging us in some way too.

Yet there's something incredibly cathartic about creation. We look at something we've created, and we're looking at an expression of ourselves. We're looking at proof, however big or small, that we're capable of creating something out of raw materials, creating something out of a vision, and turning an idea into reality.

When we realize the profundity of this experience, we realize that we can find a sense of *strength and resilience* in the experience too.

For example, I love the process of creating e-books like this one. The initial motivation is desire to produce a resource that other people can use, but, along the way, I get immense satisfaction from being able to see the project grow and take shape. It's definitely frustrating at times too (I find the editing stage in particular teeth-grittingly uncomfortable), but I always feel a sense of wonder looking at the finished product and reminding myself "I created this." Creating anything is a type of journey, and I feel proud for seeing the project through.

Regardless of the finished product, there's a lot to be said for just *creating*.

How it works

Let's start by clearing up a common myth: to get creative, you *don't* have to be artistic. Artistic skills are borne from creativity, but they are not the same as being creative. Although I enjoy creative projects, I have the drawing skills of a four-year old and seem to be missing the part of my brain that identifies which colors match and which don't. Regardless of skill, creativity is a mode of expression that's innate in all of us, so remember this if your internal dialogue starts judging your abilities.

The kind of creation you engage in will depend on your preferences, experience, curiosity, and the amount of time and money you can spend. Before choosing anything, I suggest brainstorming a list of potential creative projects. Write down everything you can think of that falls under the category of "creative." Don't censor ideas just yet, get everything down so you can come back to the list and pick out the ideas that work best for you later.

Here are some ideas to get you started:

- Writing nonfiction
- Writing fiction (including novels, plays, screenplays)
- Drawing
- Painting
- Poetry
- Cooking
- Sculpture
- Jewelry making
- Sewing
- Craftwork
- Knitting
- Textiles
- Graphic design
- Playing a musical instrument
- Singing

- Songwriting
- Collage
- Scrap booking
- Handmade gifts
- Home wares
- Furniture
- Photography
- Calligraphy
- Embroidery
- Dancing

And that list is certainly not exhaustive.

One of the great things about creative projects is that it's possible to tailor individual projects according to your budget and how much time you have. Attending evening classes or workshops are great ways to explore new creative horizons and meet others with similar interests. The internet is also a goldmine when it comes to how-tos, cheap materials, and connecting with people who have similar interests.

Why it works

There's something very special about being able to touch and hold something that you made, be it jewelry, pottery, a painting, a drawing, a wooden cabinet, or whatever project strikes your fancy.

However we choose to do it, creation is a form of self-expression, and our self-expression is an integral part of staking out our place in the world. It's an outlet for our selves and therefore an important part of self-care.

36

CHANGE YOUR SCENE

Needs: Connection, to know and be known, to see and be seen, to understand and be understood, movement and exercise, authenticity, integrity, presence, inspiration, autonomy, choice, freedom, independence, spontaneity, meaning, awareness, celebration of life, clarity, consciousness, creativity, discovery, growth, hope, learning, participation, purpose, self-expression, stimulation

Have you ever experienced *"routine depression"*?

It's what I call the following situation: in one or more areas of our lives, we imperceptibly develop a routine. This might occur before work, at work, in the evenings, or at weekends. This initial routine becomes more ingrained each day, and the "routine phenomenon" starts to spread to other areas of our life. As well as following the same routine with our work, our mornings, or our weekends, suddenly we're doing the same things in the same order every evening. We're eating the same breakfast every day, because we get exactly the same shopping at the supermarket each week. We go out on the same nights and do the same things or see the same people.

Suddenly, routine has taken over our lives. And with that, our feelings. Some people thrive living out this kind of routine, but some people experience a huge emotional cost. We start to feel flat, unmotivated, and bored, yet at the same time we might also feel threatened by the idea of changing our routines. When a friend suggests going out on a different night, we start thinking, "But I can't. Tuesdays and Saturdays are my going out nights."

So we remain: flat, unmotivated, and bored.

It's time to shift that and revitalize your week.

How it works

This one is another simple suggestion: go somewhere and do something different. Experiment with a new activity you've been wanting to try for a while, get in touch with a friend you haven't seen recently, take a different route home... Whatever you need to do to shake up your routine, do it.

These changes don't have to be dramatic; I'm not suggesting you need to walk into work on Monday morning and quit. Start with the small stuff and build up your courage. Once you begin introducing small shifts into your routines, you'll be more able to identify where you want to introduce big shifts too.

If part of you is really reluctant to give up your current routine, try incorporating new elements into it (for example, Wednesday evenings could be time dedicated to trying something new).

Why it works

Changing your routine is effective because:

1. You stop certain emotional patterns forming unconsciously—especially feelings of emptiness and mild depression.

2. You broaden the list of hobbies and activities that bring you joy, without unconsciously limiting yourself to the existing list of activities currently in your life.

3. You prevent stagnation, which can lead to us having unmet needs that we're not even aware of and, consequently, feelings of emptiness and depression.

4. We experience new places, people, and activities that we can add to our *White Lists* (more on these later in this part of the book).

37

MEDITATE

Needs: Acceptance, belonging, closeness, companionship, compassion, empathy, love, nurturing, self-respect, security, stability, to understand and be understood, safety, presence, peace, space, awareness, meaning, celebration of life, consciousness, creativity, discovery, growth, hope, learning, mourning, understanding

Meditation is one of those personal development tools that I used to mentally file under "slightly wary of this." I had tried a couple of guided meditations, but I always felt self-conscious and a bit silly.

Then I discovered Meditation Oasis (www.meditationoasis.com). The choice of meditations, the creators' approach to meditation and the fact that plenty of tracks were available for free helped my inner cynic back off. As I started to use guided meditations more regularly, something clicked; I stopped feeling self-conscious and silly and started appreciating the practice.

The beauty of meditation is that there is so much choice. You can try a guided meditation, where a narrator leads you through a mental journey using visualization, or a simple sit-and-breathe session.

In my experience, guided meditations have been incredibly helpful for exploring certain feelings or situations. On a day-to-day basis, however, the simple sit-and-breathe sessions have changed the way I view and use meditation permanently. I experimented with this kind of meditation for the first time while taking an online course led by Marianne Elliott (see the *resources page* for this book for more information).

I started Marianne's practice one December. I was getting up at 5.45am Monday to Friday and traveling to work in a different city. Each morning was dark, freezing, and grim. Spending an hour and a half on a train crammed with unhappy commuters was, unsurprisingly, affecting my mood. I had quit my job and was in the last few weeks of working out a long notice period. In addition, at that particular time, I was dealing with complications from a recent wisdom tooth removal that had made regular everyday things like eating, drinking and lying down on my left side very, very uncomfortable. I was tired, stretched, and longing for the whole period to be over.

Even though it was 5:45 a.m., even though I was freezing my ass off for the duration, and even though all I wanted to do was crawl back into bed, the ten minutes of Marianne's practice became the highlight of my day and a haven of me time early in the morning.

How it works

The practice is very simple and is most effective when done first thing in the morning:

Grab a cushion, block, or whatever you need to sit comfortably, legs crossed. Place your hands in your lap, on your thighs, or wherever feels comfortable. Alternatively, you can hold a hot cup of tea and enjoy inhaling the steam (but don't drink it during the meditation).

Set a timer to go off after 10 minutes. Start the timer, then close your eyes and focus on your breath.

You'll notice thoughts start to come up and that's OK—just let them go. If you find yourself getting involved in a train of thought, simply return your focus to your breath. You can repeat this process as many times as you need to during your 10 minutes.

You might also experience different feelings as you sit. Again, don't get involved in the thoughts that come attached to those feelings, simply focus on your breath, feel what you feel, and sit with that.

When the timer goes off, you can open your eyes and are free to get on with your day.

Once you're used to meditating for 10 minutes, you can try sitting for longer. Of course, if 10 minutes feels too long in the beginning, try sitting for 5 minutes, or even 2 minutes for the first few times. The longer you can sit, the more beneficial the practice will be. Sitting still for this time might feel uncomfortable at first. You might feel twitchy, anxious, or an array of other unpleasant sensations. This is resistance and the more you can sit with your resistance without giving in to it, the more effective (and enjoyable) your daily meditation practice will be.

Why it works

This kind of meditation is useful in a number of ways:

First, it provides us with a way to connect to our bodies and our internal experience. The longer we're able to sit and notice our feelings without getting caught up in our thoughts, the more likely it is that our true feelings will surface.

Second, this practice is great for creativity and epiphanies. During day-to-day life, our thoughts distract us, and can block new ideas, solutions, and shifts in our thinking from coming forward. When we notice those thoughts come up, but don't get attached or involved in their stories, we leave the door wide open for the thoughts and feelings underneath to emerge—which they will, in time.

Finally, another important benefit of this practice is that it teaches us how to be uncomfortable. The first few times I sat for 10 minutes, I would get to a certain point, feel sure that 10 minutes must have gone by, and that the timer on my phone had obviously just not sounded. In the beginning, I waged a daily battle with myself not to open my eyes, break the meditation, and check how much time was left—or get caught up in an internal debate about whether to do that. Eventually, I learned to trust myself (and my phone) and sit with the temptation to peek, rather than act on it or argue with myself about it.

Meditation isn't easy. As addiction specialist Dr Gabor Mate writes in his book *In the Realm of Hungry Ghosts* (North Atlantic Books, 2010): "I have a profound relationship with meditation; I think about it every day." Meditation can breed resistance but the rewards involved in sitting with that resistance and, well, sitting, are definitely worth it.

Other thoughts

Meditation is not the same as snoozing. If you happen to fall asleep, that's OK, but it probably means that a) you might not be meeting that all-important need I covered in *Sleep*, and b) you might find it helpful to keep your focus on your breath.

As I mentioned in the chapter on *Savasana*, you should be in a specific kind of relaxation, where you're calmly active and actively calm. The aim of this practice is to provide space for your thoughts and feelings, and to reconnect with yourself—not to take a power nap (you can save that for a quiet moment at work).

38

THE WHITE LISTS

The important thing is not to stop questioning. Curiosity has its own reason for existing.

—*Albert Einstein*

Needs: Connection, communication, closeness, community, love, nurturing, respect, safety, security, support, movement and exercise, rest and sleep, shelter, authenticity, integrity, presence, play, joy, peace, autonomy, choice, spontaneity, awareness, celebration of life, consciousness, creativity, discovery, effectiveness, participation, understanding

The White Lists are simple self-care tools that don't take much time and leave us with a valuable list of opportunities to enhance our self-care in the future. This suggestion builds on something we talked about in the second section of this book, when we looked at the self-care practices that are already present in your life and that already work for you. This suggestion is about making some of those practices more conscious.

How it works

To make your lists, you can either divide a single page into three columns, or use a separate sheet for each category of "people," "places," and "activities."

Next, spend twenty to thirty minutes writing down your favorites for each category. Include everything you can think of that leaves you feeling warm, fulfilled and enriched, no matter how ridiculous or mundane an item might seem. If you need one word or criterion that ties all these things together, that would be: "*wholesome.*"

Each of the items on your list should leave you feeling wholesome. It's not helpful to include things you think you should find wholesome (but don't) or things that you know deep down are a coping strategy (e.g. pouring a glass of wine to quieten lonely or restless feelings, or buying things to make yourself feel better). If in doubt, enter something onto the list with a question mark and return to it later, asking yourself whether that place or activity is wholesome, or whether it's something you've turned to in the past to mask uncomfortable feelings.

Equally the individuals on your "people" list are ideally those who support, nurture, and accept you as you are, not people you think you *should* add or *should* want to spend time with. Listen to what your gut says over your brain and go with that.

These lists won't be complete after half an hour, so to make the most of this suggestion, keep adding to your lists over the next few weeks and months, as different pleasurable people, places and activities come to mind and you discover new experiences.

Why it works

These lists have two main benefits:

1. They boost our mood in the short term. The act of compiling the lists itself reminds us of the pleasurable feelings we get from visiting these places, seeing these people, and doing these activities—without actually going, meeting, or doing any of them.

2. They provide us with a toolbox of things we can use when we want support, nurturing, or just feel like doing something that will leave us feeling fulfilled and nourished. By making these lists, we now have on hand a list of places to visit (or even just to think of) that we know will leave us feeling rejuvenated and invigorated. We have a list of people whose presence supports and nurtures us, and we have a list of activities we know we find fulfilling and refreshing.

39

SAVE THE CHANGE

Needs: Compassion, consistency empathy, nurturing, self-respect, security, safety, stability, support, trust, shelter, integrity, peace, order, autonomy, freedom, independence, awareness, clarity, competence, efficacy, growth, hope

Most of us are raised to believe that it's not polite to talk about money. But our finances are important and can say a lot about our level of self-care. Money is an emotive subject and, as we talked about in earlier chapters, is often very wrapped up in feelings around our self-worth, how much we feel we deserve, our appearance to the outside world, and notions of "success."

The fact is that money is a practical resource. Earning and having money is not a moral issue (unless you're earning it in an unethical way), but often people feel guilty about desiring or having more money than others, about wanting a raise for a job well done, about increasing their rates, and about asking for more.

Our relationship with money says a lot about our self-care. There are many self-care practices related to money I could talk about—enough to fill a whole new book—but I'm going to focus on a particular practice that I've found simple yet invaluable when it comes to financial self-care. Money is an extremely important topic when it comes to self-care, so I've also included a list of money-related resources on the resources page for this book.

In making this suggestion, I recognize everyone's financial situation is different. I've chosen this suggestion in particular, however, because it has a low barrier to entry and, over time, produces results. When you first read about it, you might hear internal voices respond with statements like, "I can't do that. I'm already living month-to-month as it is," or "I have far better things to spend my money on that this." These voices are resistance. If you feel resistance, why not make a commitment to try this suggestion for one month to see what the experience is like? You can reevaluate at the end of the month and decide whether it's something you want to continue then.

Saving money doesn't require you to start living like a monk and lead an existence devoid of fun and the occasional indulgence. Even a small amount per month is a good start, as long as it's something you do *consistently*.

Think of it like paying yourself. You expect to get paid for the work you do and would be rightfully angry if your boss came to you one month and said that by the time they'd paid all the other staff's wages, paid the office rent, the bills, and taken the head team members out for drinks a couple of times, they didn't have enough money left over to pay your salary. Sorry, but you'll have to wait until next month. Yet when it comes to savings, many of us do the same thing to ourselves: by the time we've paid our rent, our bills, our groceries, gone out a few times… oops, sorry, it doesn't look like I have enough left over this month to pay myself.

There's a really easy way to turn this around: *pay yourself first* and put something in your savings before anything else—even if it's only twenty dollars. You are worth at least that kind of commitment.

If the idea of putting even a small lump sum in your bank account each month sounds challenging, here are a couple of ways you can make it easy on yourself:

How it works: two easy ways to save

I used to set myself high savings goals that I couldn't always meet. While I felt great during the months I was able to meet my goals, my level of perfectionism around this self-imposed standard meant that I felt very demoralized and sometimes wouldn't save anything at all in a particular month if I couldn't meet my target. The internal dialogue went something like this: "I can't put in £X amount, so what's the point?" Naturally, this meant that my savings were sporadic, and I ended up feeling guilty about not meeting my own goals.

A pound (or dollar) a day

The above situation was stressful, and it really took any fun out of saving. Then I read a book called *Money Magic*, by Alvin Hall (Hodder & Stoughton Ltd, 2010). He suggested a lifetime practice of taking a pound (or a dollar) each day and putting it in a money jar. At the end of the month, take the money out of the jar and pay it straight into your bank account.

You can use this money to pay off existing debt or put it in your savings account. If you already have three to six months' worth of living expenses saved up, you can either add to your savings fund further, or use the extra cash to treat yourself to something from your wish list.

A pound or a dollar a day might not sound like much, but it equates to 365 pounds or 365 dollars over a year, which isn't insignificant. Over two years, that's an extra 730 pounds or dollars—over three, 1,095 pounds or dollars—and slightly more if you put it into a proper savings account and factor in compound interest.

Spare change

If a pound or dollar a day feels like too much, try setting up a practice where you keep your spare change. In the UK, we have £2 coins. When I was younger, my mother used to save £2 coins for a "rainy day" fund and this was a habit I continued as an adult. Every time I get a £2 coin as change, I keep it. In fact, not spending £2 coins has developed into a minor obsession: even if I don't have any other cash on me, I go out of my way to find a cash point (ATM), rather than spend one of my sacred £2 coins. Every few months, I take out my money jar and discover I've amassed £30 or so (about $50). This kind of cash can be used for whatever you want—like the dollar a day, it can go into savings or it can become your treat fund.

Last year, I discovered that my bank offers an automated online service that also helps me save incrementally using my spare change. Whenever money goes out of my bank account, my bank automatically rounds the amount up to the next full pound and deposits the difference in a separate savings account. Of course, this isn't a life-changing amount—it's anything between one pence and ninety-nine pence per transaction—however, it's another way that I add to my savings without compromising my current finances.

Why it works

How would you feel if you had an extra £1,000 tucked away in savings?

How about £5,000? £10,000? £20,000?

Pretty darn good, I imagine.

Saving money is hard right now. We're all aware of higher prices, lower interest rates, and the aftereffects of a recession. For many of us, saving is something we mean to do, know it would be good to do, but have difficulty getting around to doing.

But savings isn't just the territory of those who are well-off or high earners. It's a necessity for self-care.

The emotional relief that comes from having any kind of financial cushion in case of emergency is enormous. By saving just a little each month, you'll have much-deserved satisfaction in knowing that you're taking care of yourself both practically and emotionally.

40

TRY SOMETHING NEW

Needs: Connection, community, inclusion, nurturing, to know and be known, to see and be seen, to understand and be understood, movement/exercise, authenticity, presence, play, joy, humor, autonomy, choice, freedom, independence, space, spontaneity, meaning, awareness, celebration of life, challenge, competence, contribution, creativity, discovery, growth, hope, learning, participation, purpose, self-expression, stimulation

When we start paying attention to our levels of self-care, we open up doorways to new possibilities. Until we can hone in on what we need, what makes us tick, and what leaves us feeling fulfilled, we might not even be aware of what these things are.

Uncovering them is an exploratory process. We might be used to putting other people, other projects, or other entities (for example, a career) first. This focus on the external can leave us disconnected with ourselves and unable to identify what we really even want. If I were to ask you to list five interests or fulfilling tasks you enjoy right now, some of you might happily list 10, while others might struggle to get past two or three.

Asking ourselves what we enjoy and what we find fulfilling is all very well, but if we're out of the habit of having that kind of dialogue with ourselves, that question might be hard to answer.

An important part of self-care is reawakening the parts of ourselves that hold the key to our authentic selves—the essence of who we really are and what makes us tick.

How it works

This suggestion is about trying something new. I believe that reconnecting to experiences that are meaningful and fulfilling is an experiential process, which means it's about getting out there and *experiencing*.

This can be as intense or as relaxed as you like. You can set yourself the goal of trying something new each day, each week, or each month. The new experience can be as simple as cooking a dish you've never tried before, or as ambitious as climbing Machu Picchu.

In the beginning, start small. Initiating your discovery process with a huge goal that requires much planning, time, and money investment will feel more daunting than enlightening. Instead, do something small and often—every week if possible. You might find that doing this opens up gateways to new possibilities you hadn't even considered along the way.

Why it works

Trying new activities and experiences gives us an opportunity to pay attention to how we feel in the moment and afterwards, rather than what we *believe* we might feel. In other words, it takes us past the "thinking" level of our brain and helps us get back in touch with how we feel during certain experiences, plus what needs those experiences meet or don't meet for us. Without actually trying something, we can develop a whole series of beliefs and misconceptions that block us from activities that could be fulfilling. When we go out and try these things, we're more likely to get past the conditioned aspects of ourselves that tell us what we should and shouldn't enjoy. This helps us reconnect with our authentic experience.

A side note about experiencing

Not all new experiences are pleasant: some can be downright uncomfortable. If you come up against an uncomfortable experience, that's not necessarily a reason to shy away from it. Instead, the important question to ask is: does this leave me uncomfortable because it's not meeting my needs, or it's misaligned with my values? Or is it leaving me feeling uncomfortable because it's stretching my comfort zone, challenging beliefs I hold about myself and, ultimately, leaving me feeling vulnerable?

The former scenario is not going to serve your needs, but the latter could be an interesting opportunity for growth.

41

BEAUTIFUL PLACE VISUALIZATION

Needs: Appreciation, security, stability, safety, peace, harmony, order, space

Have you experienced olfactory memory? It goes something like this:

You walk past a hospital and the smell of disinfectant mingled with something unknown reminds you of visiting your grandfather in his care home as a child.

You enter your child's school and the smell reminds you of your own childhood schooldays.

You walk past a bakery and the smell reminds you of that trip to France, where your hotel room was directly opposite the patisserie.

We all have moments where we're taken back to somewhere from our past. In those moments, we often experience a range of memories and emotions we associate with those places. It doesn't just happen with olfaction: we can get transported to a different time and place through a range of sensory experiences—sight, sound, taste, or even just returning to a place after some time has passed. The examples above all describe times when this happens inadvertently, however we can use our powerful sensory-memory experiences as a form of self-care too.

In this suggestion, we're going to focus on sight.

How it works

Think of a place that conjures fond memories for you. It could be a childhood holiday, a certain conversation, a special moment with someone, an event, an old home, an activity, or anything else that has meaning for you. If you know a certain sensory prompt will take you back to that place—such as a certain scent or noise—try to replicate it to help the process.

Close your eyes and take yourself back to that place. In particular, focus on how you felt at that time. Let yourself feel everything: peace, excitement, joy, connection, fulfillment, serenity, anticipation, relaxation; whatever the emotions are. Let yourself experience these emotions, even if they feel slightly alien in the moment right now. Practice going to this place a few times when you're feeling comfortable in the present moment. The more times you practice going back, the easier it will be to return there whenever you need to.

Why it works

When you feel stressed, anxious, lonely, sad, or hurt, you can use this visualization as a grounding tool.

That's not the same as using it to repress so-called negative feelings: uncomfortable emotions you might be feeling in the present are important to experience and necessary to process. However, your beautiful place visualization is another self-soothing tool in your toolbox; you can return to it whenever you feel you need to. It's something that reminds us that life is in flux, the good comes with the bad, and that no matter how challenging we might find our feelings in the present, they will inevitably balance out with times of happiness and fulfillment in the past and the future.

Other thoughts

Meditation is a helpful tool we can use to create a more detailed and visceral visualization. You can find more meditation-related links and tools on the resources page for this book (www.becomingwhoyouare.net/fctt-resources).

42

ASK FOR IT

A dishonest yes is a no to yourself.

—Byron Katie

Needs: Acceptance, belonging, communication, consideration, empathy, inclusion, intimacy, mutuality, respect and self-respect, honesty, authenticity, integrity, presence, ease, equality, autonomy, choice, freedom, independence, clarity, consciousness, participation, self-expression

As I've already mentioned a few times during this book, the conventional notions of self-care are far from the reality of what self-care really means. We've looked at how a large part of self-care revolves around our relationship with ourselves. In this suggestion, we're going one step further and looking at how a large part of our self-care involves *how we relate to other people* too.

We need relationships and community to survive, yet they are often one of the biggest causes of unrest and dis-ease in our lives. Conflicting needs and desires vie for attention, presidency, and importance. Old family patterns, beliefs, and roles rear up, provoked by group settings and dynamics. In times of strife, we psychologically regress. This could be either back to the helpless children we once were, depending on the other person or people to meet our needs, or to a harsh parental role, negating or minimizing the other person's needs and feelings.

These dynamics are complicated and can start to dominate our interactions with others. When we get stuck in these dynamics, it is they, rather than our desire to get our needs met, that dominates.

The truth is, *we are the only people that can take action to meet our needs.*

Stay with this sentence for a moment and just let that sink in. Think about what it means for you and your life right now.

You are the only one that can meet your needs. You, and only you, have a responsibility to meet your own needs, just as other people have a responsibility to meet theirs. This suggestion is about helping you effectively meet your own needs in relation to other people.

How it works

The fact that we're responsible for meeting our own needs doesn't mean that we don't need other people as part of that process. There will be times when we need support, compassion, acceptance, reassurance, and more from external sources. And in those times, the only way to give ourselves a good chance of meeting those needs is to do something that makes many people cringe with discomfort:

Ask for it.

Perhaps that sounds simple, doable and nothing new to you. Perhaps, you know it's healthy, but you struggle to put it into practice. Perhaps the notion of asking for something and asserting your needs feels too threatening to your relationships as they currently stand. What if people minimize, reject or scorn them? What happens to your needs then?

We'll talk about that in a moment, but first let's return to that crucial statement.

Ask for it.

It sounds simple but, for many people, being open and assertive about what you need right now is one of the most challenging and vulnerable things you could do.

Assertiveness and negotiation are huge topics. They're not just the domain of the business world—they're necessary topics in a book about self-care. After all, how can we get our needs met if we can't express what those needs are and make requests?

As much as we might want them to be, *other people are not mind readers*. If we want to care for ourselves, we have to be willing to ask for what we want and need, even if doing so leaves us feeling uncomfortable. This includes needs like respect and compassion, as well as needs for distance, alone time and an assertion of preferred boundaries.

Of course, this is easier said than done. This suggestion assumes we're *aware of* what we want and need enough to be able to make these requests. I hope that you can use some of the other suggestions in this book to become more aware of what you need, and you can use this suggestion to communicate that to other people. If we've lost touch with our needs, reconnecting to them can take time, but it will happen if you give them the space to come forward.

What if others can't meet or even respect your needs? It's a scary prospect, but when that happens, the world simply keeps turning. We are not obligated to meet others' needs and they are not obligated to meet ours. At the same moment we have needs we would like to meet, so do they, and sometimes these needs conflict. I might have a need for companionship, connection and closeness, and the person I make a request of to meet those needs might, at that moment, have a need for solitude and peace.

At the same time, if someone outright rejects or belittles our needs, it burns. It can plant the seeds of self-doubt ("Should I really need this right now?"), it can leave us questioning our self-knowledge, our awareness, our normalcy as a human being, whether we fit into the human race, and whether we are acceptable. This is all heavy stuff.

Although it's easier said than remembered, these interactions are insightful. Surrounding ourselves with people who are respectful and accepting of our needs—even if they can't meet them—is one of our most important acts of self-care (remember *Connection*?). When someone rejects your needs, scorns them, belittles them, or fails to accept their existence, it has everything to do with them and nothing to do with you. It shows where they are in their own journey and perhaps demonstrates the struggles they face with accepting their own needs too. People who repeatedly treat your needs in this way are not earning your time or a place close to the center of your life.

Distancing yourself from people who reject your needs to make room for those who welcome them with acceptance and recognition is one of the most challenging aspects of self-care. In the long term, it's also one of the most beneficial and rewarding. It can cause a huge amount of personal upheaval, it can piss people off, and it can lead to downright uncomfortable conversations. After all, you're breaking a pattern. But when we truly care about ourselves, we want people around us who care about our needs. To make room for these people, we need to find space away from those who don't.

It can be hard to identify our needs in any given moment, especially as we explore this idea for the first time and allow ourselves to feel and acknowledge what might have been buried for many years. Like *Nonviolent Communication*, a good place to start is to check in with yourself at different points during each day and ask: "How am I feeling right now? What am I needing right now?"

The answers might be clear, they might be "I have no idea." All skills take practice though, and the more times you answer "I have no idea," the closer you are to the day when you start answering "I think I feel sad," "I feel elated," "I feel angry," and "I feel relieved."

Do what you need to do to make this question a part of your everyday life. Create a habit that sees you asking yourself first thing in the morning and last thing at night. Set a timer on your phone or computer that goes off four or five times each day. Practice, practice, practice, and you'll find that all the answers you need are there.

Why it works

As someone who can struggle with assertiveness and negotiation, I know all too well that expressing our needs to others can feel uncomfortable, and that it might never be something that feels natural or comes easily. Whatever kind of reaction you receive from someone when you express your needs, what counts is that you've taken that step and demonstrated to yourself that your needs are important.

As I explain above, it's difficult to know how we can meet our needs without being able to make requests of other people. Whatever the response, as long as we are willing to acknowledge, accept and assert our needs, we are demonstrating to ourselves that:

A) It is acceptable to want support from other people and ask them for support in our self-care journey.

B) We can negotiate how to effectively meet everyone's needs. It's not a win-lose situation.

And:

C) Our needs are important enough to have a voice, not just internally but among the people who are part of our inner circle too.

43

WALL YOUR TIME

Needs: Self-respect, support, movement and exercise, rest and sleep, authenticity, integrity, play, joy, peace, autonomy, choice, freedom, independence, space, spontaneity, awareness, consciousness, creativity, discovery, efficacy, effectiveness, growth, learning, purpose, self-expression

In *Ask for it*, we started talking about the idea of boundaries. In that context, it was boundaries with other people. In this suggestion, we are talking about boundaries with ourselves—or, more specifically, parts of ourselves.

This suggestion is about asserting your need for downtime and relaxation—or whatever else it is you need—with yourself.

How it works

One of the most effective ways I've found of doing this is to "wall my time."

When walling your time, make it concrete. Sit down with your calendar or diary and physically block out as much time as you think you'll need for yourself. This might sound a little rigid, but there's a good reason for it. Remember that Parkinson's Law says that a task expands to fit the time available. If you don't wall your time and stick to it, your other commitments will overwhelm the time you want to use for yourself. If you consciously block out time for yourself, you're far more likely to honor that time than if you start the week assuming that an hour or more will magically appear at some point—it won't.

If you know that you struggle to find the time to engage in self-care activities, or even just to relax, walling your time is a simple way of committing as much time as you need to yourself each week. Once you've blocked off the time, stick to it. You might experience unexpected situations or emergencies that mean you can't

---

honor the commitment but, as long as you show up for yourself more often than not, you send the message to yourself that you're worth this time. And if you find that "emergencies" start to get in the way of your self-appointment on a regular basis, this might be a sign that you need to reevaluate what counts as an emergency in your book and where your self-care falls on your list of priorities.

Remember that you are the one person, and this is the one body, that's going to travel with you through life. Taking care of that person and body, nurturing it and giving it time to replenish, restock and regenerate might not feel more important than the 101 other things you have to do in any given day, but the time you take for yourself will be far more beneficial to you in the long term than staying a couple of hours extra at work that evening, avoiding assertiveness, or sacrificing your self-care for what feels like the path of least resistance.

And once you have that time... it's yours, to do whatever you like. Select from the other self-care suggestions in this book, take a walk, read your favorite novel, sleep, meditate, just lie there, or wait and see what strikes your fancy in the moment. Whatever you do, don't do anything that feels like an obligation, a chore, something you should be doing with the time, or something that leaves you feeling "blah." That's the beauty of this time: it's yours, to spend on yourself.

The world can, and will, wait.

Why it works

Walling your time can be particularly useful if you work for yourself, have a demanding job, or hold many responsibilities—for example, as a caregiver or parent. When we have these external demands and responsibilities, we can struggle to set healthy boundaries around these activities. This leaves us with little time for ourselves, our relationships and regeneration.

This is where our assertiveness and boundaries come in. Walling your time requires that you set clear boundaries around time for yourself, and that you are assertive with your partner, boss, colleagues, clients, and whoever else you need to be assertive with that this is *your* time.

Above all else, the number one person you need to be assertive with is *yourself.* Parts of you will resist this suggestion, resist being assertive, and resist daring to set aside a certain amount of time per week just for you. If you have a particularly vocal internal taskmaster, that part will probably have a *lot* to say about your decision.

Walling your time requires invoking the parts of you that are nurturing, strong, and assertive with your critics, internal and external. These nurturing parts will need to stand up for you and protect the more vulnerable, guilt-prone parts from external and internal influences.

44

AFFIRMATIONS

Needs: Acceptance, affection, appreciation, connection, compassion, empathy, nurturing, respect/self-respect, safety, security, support, authenticity, integrity, presence, independence, meaning, awareness, celebration of life, challenge, clarity, competence, consciousness, contribution, creativity, discovery, efficacy, effectiveness, growth, hope, learning, purpose, self-expression, stimulation, to matter, understanding

I'm the first person to raise an eyebrow when I hear the word "affirmation." For me, this term conjures up images of people standing in front of their bathroom mirror in the morning, pulling fierce faces while repeating "I'm a tiger, I'm a tiger."

No thanks.

Over the last few years, however, I've discovered that affirmations don't have to be cheesy. They don't have to make you cringe. Instead, they can be incredibly helpful when it comes to rewriting beliefs and thought patterns.

How it works

One of the great things about affirmations is they can take whatever form you want. Standing in front of my mirror repeating "I'm a strong, confident and empowered young woman" isn't my cup of tea, but that doesn't mean it won't work for you. The most important thing is to find or create a set of affirmations that resonate with you. These might be general affirmations, or affirmations around certain topics, such as money, love, relationships, self-worth, and work.

Affirmations are based in truth. If I'm 200 pounds overweight, it's not going to be particularly helpful for me to tell myself "I am slim and athletic" (nor will it help me address the reasons I'm 200 pounds overweight to begin with). Instead, it might be more helpful to focus on shifting my self-concept to one that includes the *possibility* of meeting that vision (if that is what I want, of course). This might look something like, "I give myself permission to take care of my body" or "I am worthy of doing what is best for my body and my quality of life."

Even if you've never engaged with affirmations in the past, you know which affirmations will work best for you right now. To get you started, here are some suggestions:

1. I have everything I need to lead the life I want

2. I am enough, just as I am

3. I am worthy of love and acceptance, just as I am

4. I can be both strong and vulnerable

5. I have my permission to live the life I want and fulfill the dreams I have

And, taken from Part 1:

6. I am understandable, I am relatable, I am acceptable

Why it works

If you've either read the book or seen the film version of *The Help*, you'll remember Aibileen repeating to Mae Mobley "You is kind. You is smart. You is important." We understand the importance of her words and the gift those sentences hold for an abused child. We understand that her affirmations are powerful, and we hope that Mae Mobley can take these words to heart and hold on to them, even when her mother and father are communicating the opposite.

Those scenes are a great example of why affirmations can be so helpful. Affirmations are short, meaningful statements. If, like me in the past, you think affirmations aren't for you, you might be surprised to learn you already have a head full of them. Although affirmations have gained a reputation as the territory of New Age gurus and crowd-pleasing self-help celebrities, they are no different from the thousands of thoughts that run through our minds every day.

For example, if you have a vocal inner critic, you might recognize the following statements:

"You're not good enough."

"[Insert name here] is smarter/prettier/better than you."

"You're too quiet."

"You're too boring."

"You don't offer as much value as other people."

"If you do [insert activity here], people will judge or laugh at you."

We all experience statements like these at some point or another and, when we do, what we're experiencing is a negative type of affirmation. Positive affirmations are designed to replace those thoughts with positive, encouraging, and accepting statements. They prevent the voice of doom taking over, and replace self-attacking or self-defeating thoughts with thoughts that are fairer and based more on objective reality.

Another way to think about affirmations is that they help you to replace a strong critical voice with a strong nurturing voice. When you dare to dream, affirmations help replace "You couldn't possibly do that.... Who do you think you are?" with "Yes, you could do that ... *because* of who you are."

They replace all the reasons why you can't do something, be something, and deserve something, with all the reasons you can and do.

PART 6

Continuing the Journey

45

HOW TO USE THESE SUGGESTIONS

As we reach the end of this book, you might be thinking "OK, so how do I use all of these practices? When do I do them, how often do I do them, who do I do them with?"

The answers to all of these questions are your decision and yours alone.

I know: it would be much easier if someone created a universal self-care plan that took away any and all responsibility from us as individuals and told us what we should do and when we should do it for maximum need-meeting and all-round well-being.

But we're all very different people with different needs, and I'm not going to intrude on your individuality, your background, your current circumstances, or your desires by telling you how you should be doing your self-care. You are more than capable of doing this yourself.

Although I don't believe it's my place to prescribe self-care in metered doses, I do want to share a few suggestions I've found helpful when it comes to my own self-care. I hope they help you too.

Schedule it in

Self-care doesn't just happen—you need to make time for it. Prioritize your self-care as you would any other appointment or commitment. You write down doctor's appointments, meetings, and take steps to remember places and times that involve other people, so show yourself the same courtesy.

Use the needs list

If you haven't already made the list from *Part 2: Starting with the Present*, go back and do it now. The more you practice identifying what your needs are and which self-care practices will help you meet those needs, the more effective your overall self-care practice will be. No matter how much resistance you feel to making the list right now, it will serve you well long into the future.

Learn about your chatter

Practice noticing the internal chatter you experience around self-care, especially any resistant or negative voices. The more aware we can become of this dialogue, the less our internal chatter will control us.

Slow it down

Identifying our needs is hard when we're not used to thinking about ourselves in that way (i.e. as a human). Developing this skill is akin to learning a foreign language: no one is going to walk out of one French lesson as a fluent conversationalist. It takes time, practice, mistakes, and did I mention time? When I started thinking in needs-based language, it felt clumsy, awkward, and contrived. I felt like an impostor. Over time, however, the awkwardness imperceptibly shifted into something that felt more natural. Eventually it became the default way I thought about myself and other people around me.

Wherever you are in your self-care journey, you have everything you need to meet your own needs. When I look at how much my relationship with myself and my experience of the world around me has shifted over the last several years, I am amazed by how much better I behave towards myself and relate to myself now.

We all start from different places but I promise you: if I can do it, you can certainly do it, too.

46

THANK YOU FOR READING

Thanks for reading *From Coping to Thriving*. I hope you enjoyed it and that it's provided you with ideas and inspiration for deepening your self-care practice.

If you enjoyed this book, I'd be really grateful if you could take a couple of minutes to leave a review on Amazon. Sharing your thoughts is helpful to other potential readers, and your feedback helps me improve as an author.

You can find a living list of resources that builds on and enhances some of the content in this book over at my website, Becoming Who You Are (www.becomingwhoyouare.net/fctt-resources). As I come across new self-care related resources, I'll keep updating the list and I'd also love to hear if you have any suggestions of your own.

At Becoming Who You Are, you can find information, tips and resources that enable you to create the life you want from the inside out using rational personal development. You can also sign up to receive your free ebook on *The Five Most Common Blocks to Authenticity... and How to Overcome Them*.

If you'd like to get in touch with any questions, comments or to talk about your experience with self-care, please email me at hannah@becomingwhoyouare.net.

Until next time, take care.

Appendix: List of Activities Organized by Need

Acceptance: Good Food, Remember to Breathe, Connection, H.A.L.T, Yoga, Laughter, Savasana, Create a Self-care Kit, Create a Mini-Retreat, Write a Letter to Your Future Self, Nonviolent Communication, Journaling, Meditate, Ask For It, Affirmations,

Affection: Good Food, Connection, Create a Self-care Kit, Create a Mini-Retreat, Treat List, Write a Letter to Your Future Self, Nonviolent Communication, Affirmations,

Air: Remember to Breathe, H.A.L.T, Savasana

Appreciation: Connection, Laughter, Create a Self-care Kit, Create a Mini-Retreat, Treat List, Write a Letter to Your Future Self, Journaling, Beautiful Place Visualization, Affirmations,

Authenticity: Connection, Time Charts, Laughter, Party Like It's 1999, Create a Self-care Kit, Create a Mini-Retreat, Treat List, Create Unplanned Time, Nonviolent Communication, Journaling, Create Something, Change Your Scene, The White Lists, Try Something New, Wall Your Time, Ask For It, Affirmations,

Autonomy: Time Charts, Create a Self-care Kit, Create a Mini-Retreat, Treat List, Create Unplanned Time, Change Your Scene, The White Lists, Save the Change, Try Something New, Wall Your Time, Ask For It,

Awareness: Sleep, Good Food, Remember to Breathe, Time Charts, Yoga, Remember to Breathe, Time Charts, Savasana, Relieving Tension, Create a Self-care Kit, Nonviolent Communication, Quote Bank, Journaling, Change Your Scene, Meditate, The White Lists, Save the Change, Try Something New, Wall Your Time, Affirmations,

Beauty: Yoga, Create Something

Belonging: Exercise, Connection, Laughter, Relieving Tension, Nonviolent Communication, Meditate, Ask For It,

Celebration of life: Good Food, Remember to Breathe, Time Charts, Yoga, Laughter, Savasana, Party Like It's 1999, Create a Mini-

Retreat, Treat List, Write a Letter to Your Future Self, Create Something, Change Your Scene, Meditate, The White Lists, Try Something New, Affirmations,

Challenge: Exercise, Yoga, Create Something, Try Something New, Affirmations,

Choice: Good Food, Time Charts, R-E-L-A-X, Create Unplanned Time, Change Your Scene, The White Lists, Try Something New, Wall Your Time, Ask For It,

Clarity: Sleep, Time Charts, Yoga, Create a Mini-Retreat, Quote Bank, Journaling, Change Your Scene, Save the Change, Ask For It, Affirmations,

Closeness: Remember to Breathe, Connection, Laughter, Savasana, Relieving Tension, Create a Self-care Kit, Nonviolent Communication, Journaling, Meditate, The White Lists,

Communication: Connection, Laughter, Write a Letter to Your Future Self, Nonviolent Communication, Quote Bank, The White Lists, Try Something New, Ask For It,

Community: Connection, Yoga, Laughter, The White Lists, Try Something New,

Companionship: Good Food, Connection, Laughter, Write a Letter to Your Future Self, Quote Bank, Journaling, Meditate,

Compassion: Good Food, Remember to Breathe, Connection, H.A.L.T, Time Charts, R-E-L-A-X, Yoga, Laughter, Savasana, Relieving Tension, Create a Self-care Kit, Create a Mini-Retreat, Treat List, Write a Letter to Your Future Self, Nonviolent Communication, Quote Bank, Journaling, Meditate, Save the Change, Affirmations,

Competence: Yoga, Create Something, Save the Change, Try Something New, Affirmations,

Connection: H.A.L.T, Time Charts, Write a Letter to Your Future Self, Create Unplanned Time, Nonviolent Communication, Quote Bank, Create Something, Change Your Scene, The White Lists, Affirmations,

Consciousness: Sleep, Good Food, Remember to Breathe, Time Charts, R-E-L-A-X, Yoga, Savasana, Relieving Tension, Write a Letter to Your Future Self, Nonviolent Communication, Quote Bank, Journaling, Change Your Scene, Meditate, The White Lists, Wall Your Time, Ask For It, Affirmations,

Consistency: Good Food, Connection, Time Charts, Create a Self-care Kit, Treat List, Save the Change

Consideration: Good Food, Connection, Time Charts, R-E-L-A-X, Create a Self-care Kit, Create a Mini-Retreat, Treat List, Write a Letter to Your Future Self, Nonviolent Communication, Ask For It,

Contribution: Exercise, Create Something, Try Something New, Affirmations,

Cooperation: Connection, Nonviolent Communication

Creativity: Write a Letter to Your Future Self, Create Unplanned Time, Quote Bank, Journaling, Create Something, Change Your Scene, Meditate, The White Lists, Try Something New, Wall Your Time, Affirmations,

Discovery: Time Charts, Yoga, Create a Mini-Retreat, Write a Letter to Your Future Self, Create Unplanned Time, Journaling, Change Your Scene, Meditate, The White Lists, Try Something New, Wall Your Time, Affirmations,

Ease: Sleep, R-E-L-A-X, Yoga, Ask For It,

Efficacy: Sleep, Time Charts, Write a Letter to Your Future Self, Nonviolent Communication, Quote Bank, Create Something, Save the Change, Wall Your Time, Affirmations,

Effectiveness: Sleep, H.A.L.T, Time Charts, Write a Letter to Your Future Self, Nonviolent Communication, Quote Bank, Create Something, The White Lists, Wall Your Time, Affirmations,

Empathy: Connection, H.A.L.T, Time Charts, R-E-L-A-X, Yoga, Savasana, Create a Self-care Kit, Create a Mini-Retreat, Write a Letter to Your Future Self, Nonviolent Communication, Quote Bank, Journaling, Meditate, Save the Change, Ask For It, Affirmations,

Equality: Nonviolent Communication, Ask For It,

Food: Good Food, H.A.L.T

Freedom: Good Food, Time Charts, R-E-L-A-X, Laughter, Party Like It's 1999, Create Unplanned Time, Create Something, Change Your Scene, Save the Change, Try Something New, Wall Your Time, Ask For It,

Growth: Exercise, Connection, Time Charts, Yoga, Create a Self-care Kit, Create a Mini-Retreat, Write a Letter to Your Future Self, Create Unplanned Time, Nonviolent Communication, Quote Bank, Journaling, Create Something, Change Your Scene, Meditate, Save the Change, Try Something New, Wall Your Time, Affirmations,

Harmony: Good Food, Yoga, Write a Letter to Your Future Self, Nonviolent Communication, Beautiful Place Visualization,

Honesty: Time Charts, Write a Letter to Your Future Self, Create Unplanned Time, Nonviolent Communication, Journaling, Ask For It,

Hope: Yoga, Create a Mini-Retreat, Write a Letter to Your Future Self, Quote Bank, Journaling, Change Your Scene, Meditate, Save the Change, Try Something New, Affirmations,

Humor: Laughter, Party Like It's 1999, Try Something New,

Inclusion: Connection, Laughter, Create a Mini-Retreat, Try Something New, Ask For It,

Independence: Time Charts, Create Unplanned Time, Nonviolent Communication, Change Your Scene, Save the Change, Try Something New, Wall Your Time, Ask For It, Affirmations,

Inspiration: Create a Mini-Retreat, Quote Bank, Create Something, Change Your Scene,

Integrity: Connection, Time Charts, Create Unplanned Time, Nonviolent Communication, Journaling, Change Your Scene, The White Lists, Save the Change, Wall Your Time, Ask For It, Affirmations,

Intimacy: Connection, Laughter, Savasana, Create a Self-care Kit, Create a Mini-Retreat, Nonviolent Communication, Journaling, Ask For It,

Joy: Time Charts, Laughter, Party Like It's 1999, Write a Letter to Your Future Self, Create Something, The White Lists, Try Something New, Wall Your Time,

Learning: Exercise, Connection, Yoga, Create a Mini-Retreat, Write a Letter to Your Future Self, Create Unplanned Time, Nonviolent Communication, Quote Bank, Journaling, Create Something, Change Your Scene, Meditate, Try Something New, Wall Your Time, Affirmations,

Love: Remember to Breathe, Connection, Savasana, Create a Self-care Kit, Create a Mini-Retreat, Treat List, Write a Letter to Your Future Self, Meditate, The White Lists,

Meaning: Connection, Write a Letter to Your Future Self, Journaling, Change Your Scene, Meditate, Try Something New, Affirmations,

Movement and exercise: Exercise, Yoga, Party Like It's 1999, Create a Mini-Retreat, Change Your Scene, The White Lists, Try Something New, Wall Your Time,

Mourning: Create a Mini-Retreat, Journaling, Meditate,

Mutuality: Connection, Laughter, Nonviolent Communication, Ask For It,

Nurturing: Good Food, Remember to Breathe, Connection, H.A.L.T, Time Charts, Yoga, Laughter, Savasana, Relieving Tension, Create a Self-care Kit, Create a Mini-Retreat, Treat List, Write a Letter to Your Future Self, Nonviolent Communication, Journaling, Meditate, The White Lists, Save the Change, Try Something New, Affirmations,

Order: Time Charts, Nonviolent Communication, Save the Change, Beautiful Place Visualization,

Participation: Exercise, Connection, Yoga, Laughter, Party Like It's 1999, Nonviolent Communication, Create Something, Change Your Scene, The White Lists, Try Something New, Ask For It,

Peace: Savasana, Relieving Tension, Create a Self-care Kit, Create a Mini-Retreat, Treat List, Create Unplanned Time, Nonviolent Communication, Quote Bank, Meditate, The White Lists, Save the Change, Beautiful Place Visualization, Wall Your Time,

Play: Exercise, Time Charts, Laughter, Party Like It's 1999, Create a Self-care Kit, Treat List, Create Unplanned Time, Create Something, The White Lists, Try Something New, Wall Your Time,

Presence: Sleep, Remember to Breathe, Connection, H.A.L.T, Time Charts, Yoga, Laughter, Savasana, Party Like It's 1999, Create a Self-care Kit, Create a Mini-Retreat, Create Unplanned Time, Nonviolent Communication, Create Something, Change Your Scene, The White Lists, Try Something New, Ask For It, Affirmations,

Purpose: Time Charts, Yoga, Create Unplanned Time, Create Something, Change Your Scene, Try Something New, Wall Your Time, Affirmations,

Respect: Nonviolent Communication, The White Lists, Ask For It, Affirmations,

Rest and sleep: Sleep, H.A.L.T, Time Charts, Savasana, Relieving Tension, Create a Mini-Retreat, The White Lists, Wall Your Time,

Safety: Connection, Create a Mini-Retreat, Journaling, Meditate, The White Lists, Save the Change, Beautiful Place Visualization, Affirmations,

Security: Remember to Breathe, Connection, Savasana, Nonviolent Communication, Journaling, Meditate, The White Lists, Save the Change, Beautiful Place Visualization, Affirmations,

Self-expression: Connection, Yoga, Laughter, Party Like It's 1999, Create a Self-care Kit, Create a Mini-Retreat, Write a Letter to Your Future Self, Create Unplanned Time, Nonviolent Communication, Journaling, Create Something, Change Your Scene, Try Something New, Wall Your Time, Ask For It, Affirmations,

Self-respect: Exercise, Good Food, Remember to Breathe, H.A.L.T, Time Charts, R-E-L-A-X, Yoga, Savasana, Relieving Tension, Create a Self-care Kit, Create a Mini-Retreat, Treat List, Write a Letter to Your Future Self, Quote Bank, Journaling, Meditate, Save the Change, Wall Your Time, Ask For It, Affirmations,

Shelter: The White Lists, Save the Change,

Space: Remember to Breathe, Time Charts, R-E-L-A-X, Yoga, Savasana, Relieving Tension, Create a Self-care Kit, Create a Mini-Retreat, Create Unplanned Time, Nonviolent Communication, Journaling, Meditate, Try Something New, Beautiful Place Visualization, Wall Your Time,

Spontaneity: Exercise, Time Charts, Laughter, Party Like It's 1999, Create Unplanned Time, Create Something, Change Your Scene, The White Lists, Try Something New, Wall Your Time,

Stability: Remember to Breathe, Connection, H.A.L.T, Time Charts, Savasana, Meditate, Save the Change, Beautiful Place Visualization,

Stimulation: Exercise, Connection, Yoga, Laughter, Party Like It's 1999, Create a Mini-Retreat, Nonviolent Communication, Quote Bank, Journaling, Create Something, Change Your Scene, Try Something New, Affirmations,

Support: Connection, H.A.L.T, Time Charts, Create a Self-care Kit, Create a Mini-Retreat, Create Unplanned Time, Nonviolent Communication, Quote Bank, Journaling, The White Lists, Save the Change, Wall Your Time, Affirmations,

To know and be known: Connection, H.A.L.T, Time Charts, Nonviolent Communication, Quote Bank, Journaling, Create Something, Change Your Scene, Try Something New,

To matter: Connection, H.A.L.T, Create a Self-care Kit, Create a Mini-Retreat, Treat List, Write a Letter to Your Future Self, Affirmations,

To see and be seen: Connection, Laughter, Nonviolent Communication, Quote Bank, Journaling, Create Something, Change Your Scene, Try Something New,

To understand and be understood: Connection, Create a Mini-Retreat, Nonviolent Communication, Quote Bank, Journaling, Change Your Scene, Meditate, Try Something New,

Touch: Connection, Create a Mini-Retreat

Trust: Connection, H.A.L.T, Create Unplanned Time, Nonviolent Communication, Save the Change,

Understanding: Good Food, Remember to Breathe, Time Charts, Savasana, Write a Letter to Your Future Self, Create Unplanned Time, Nonviolent Communication, Quote Bank, Journaling, Meditate, The White Lists, Affirmations,

Warmth: Connection, Yoga, Relieving Tension, Nonviolent Communication

Water: Good Food, H.A.L.T, Laughter

About the Author

Hannah Braime is an author and coach from London, England. She is the founder of Becoming Who You Are (www.becomingwhoyouare.net), where she shares practical psychology-based articles, tools and resources on living with greater courage, compassion and authenticity.

You can continue your personal growth journey and get access to free workbooks, audios and book summaries by joining the Becoming Who You Are Library here: http://bit.ly/BWYAlibrary

Connect with Hannah online:

Email: hannah@becomingwhoyouare.net
Website: www.becomingwhoyouare.net
Facebook: www.facebook.com/becomingwhoyouare
Pinterest: www.pinterest.com/hannahbraime

Other Books by Hannah Braime

The Ultimate Guide to Journaling

In *The Ultimate Guide to Journaling*, you'll find the tips, inspiration, and prompts you need to start and maintain a journaling practice for DIY self-discovery. This clear and concise handbook shares everything you need to know to deepen your relationship with yourself using this powerful personal development tool. Covering foundational topics like how to journal, which tools to use, and how to make it a regular habit, as well as over 30 different journaling techniques and many more prompts, The Ultimate Guide to Journaling will help you keep your practice flowing for years to come. Through a combination of handwritten, digital and art journaling suggestions, you'll learn how to tap into your internal resources, learn more about what makes you who you are, discover how to negotiate with the different parts of yourself, and create a safe space to explore your inner world.

Available through Amazon for Kindle, paperback and audiobook (visit http://amzn.to/1XfSFfy to purchase), plus all other major ebook retailers.

Acknowledgements

Although I wrote the drafts of this book, the final product was a collaborative effort and would have been a very different book without help and support from others.

Thanks to the many writers and speakers who have been courageous enough to share their work with the world and have had a huge impact on this book.

Much appreciation and gratitude to everyone who reads and supports Becoming Who You Are; your questions and comments shaped the book and I'm constantly touched by your feedback, support, and stories.

Thanks to Will Moyer for creating a beautiful cover and for moral support.

Heartfelt thanks to the beta readers: Rose, Becca, Sarah, Jess, Deborah, Tom, Jack, Bruce, Jacqueline, and Rebecca. The book is a million times better thanks to your input and I'm incredibly grateful for your feedback, suggestions, and grammar lessons! Extra special thanks to Cheryl for her time, patience and useful guidance.

Finally, thanks to Jake for reading more iterations of this book than I can count, for encouragement, enthusiasm, and your support in life. You inspire me to be the best version of myself.

Printed in Great Britain
by Amazon